Communicate Clearly, Confidently & Credibly

Leading Authorities Share Their Best
Communication Secrets so
You Can Enjoy Stronger Relationships,
Greater Respect & Renewed Self-Assurance.

Compiled by Doug Smart

James &
Brookfield

J&B

Publishers

Communicate Clearly, Confidently & Credibly

Managing Editor: Gayle Smart

Editor: Sara Kahan
Book Designer: Paula Chance
Copyright ©2004

Disclaimer: This book is a compilation of ideas from numerous experts who have each contributed a chapter. As such, the views expressed in each chapter are those of the authors and not necessarily the views of James & Brookfield Publishers.

For more information, contact:
James & Brookfield Publishers
P.O. Box 768024
Roswell, GA 30076

Library of Congress Catalog Number in Publication Data

ISBN: 0-9749191-4-4

10 9 8 7 6 5 4 3 2 1

TABLE OF CONTENTS

TARGET TALK:™
How to Trigger Positive Responses and Get Things Done In an Inattentive World

by Connie Dieken

I first noticed the phenomenon in the studio of our daily television talk show. We interviewed prominent guests, such as the president of the United States, Michael J. Fox, Dr. Ruth, and Richard Simmons. On any given day, the studio sparkled with energy and stimulating exchanges.

Yet as these celebrities appeared in the flesh, our in-studio audiences weren't watching the live action unfolding in front of their noses. Instead, they transfixed on something else: the *television monitors.* They chose to gaze right past the real interaction and zero in on our guests' flickering images on TV. I was both amazed and perplexed.

Turns out, I witnessed an emerging trend at its start: people tuning out actual interaction in favor of electronic contact. What I observed was a clear signal of the new dynamics of communication, which is now compounded by cell phones, PDAs, Blackberries, and round-the-clock Internet habits. Clearly, our communication channels have been powerfully reprogrammed.

This new dynamic is radically altering our face-to-face interactions. By shifting our attention from humans to electronics, our in-the-flesh communication skills are plummeting. Our ability to attract and hold people's attention is slipping faster than a New York minute. When we do talk nose-to-nose, we're sabotaging our careers with impatience, inappropriate comments, revealing body language, and the illusion that we're actually getting through to people.

The situation has gone beyond attention deficit disorder. It's now attention *denial* disorder. You have to work hard to earn someone's attention for even one minute. Participants in my communication workshops lament that it's a daunting challenge to deal directly and satisfactorily with inattentive people.

We're experiencing societal conditions significantly different from any before. We'll commit career sabotage if we expect our old interaction stand-bys to cut through today's communication clutter.

Have you noticed that people now tune you out in an instant? It's as if everyone you talk to has a remote control implanted in their brain, passing instant judgments and clicking you off in seconds.

Maybe you're doing it, too. How many devices do you cram into your briefcase or purse to communicate with invisible people?

What's inside your briefcase?

- Cell phone
- Pager
- Laptop
- PDA
- Blackberry
- Combo phone & PDA

Don't get me wrong; I use these communication tools every day. They offer mobility, efficiency, speed, and contact with family and clients. However, overuse (and the accompanying plunge in face-to-face dealings) poses the risk of emotional disconnect from live interaction. For example, at an airport recently, amidst the outbreak of ringing, shrieking, vibrating, beeping, musically-charged devices, I observed travelers disregarding their family and co-workers seated next to them to reveal amazingly private information to unseen people. In ten minutes, I overheard:

- A young man argue a pre-nuptial agreement with his fiancée
- A woman divulge where her house key is hidden
- A baby boomer reveal his name, street address and social security number
- A mother explain how to change a diaper, in dirty detail.

Have you experienced similar situation? Of course you have.

Venture almost anywhere and you're bound to absorb intensely personal information, delivered in piercing voices from people who don't seem to care that everyone in earshot is forced to eavesdrop. It's become a new norm to reveal private information in public—so long as you're not actually chatting face-to-face. Heaven forbid you communicate openly with the person next to you.

So how can you compete with these distractions that are changing the face of interactions? I left my career in front of the camera to research communication dynamics and uncover the best way to get through to people in today's inattentive society. I've derived a simple yet uniquely potent methodology called Target Talk™. It's a step-by-step process to cut through communication clutter, trigger buy-in, and generate positive actions. This formula provides a framework in which to base all your communications: presentations, phone calls, voice-mails, live interaction, meetings, and e-mail. Here's how it works:

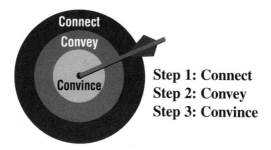

Step 1: Connect
Step 2: Convey
Step 3: Convince

Step 1: Connect

Communication is a contact sport. It requires constant attention and adjustments. The first step is to fully connect with people. Focus on others' needs and concerns, and they'll return the favor by allowing you access to their time and emotions. Plug in to people before you launch into whatever you want them to do, think, or buy. You're spinning your wheels if you expect people to concentrate on you without a compelling personal benefit. Instead, connect the dots—you'll win buy-in by engaging and laying out your listeners' advantages early on. Here are three tactics for making connections:

1. Create chemistry

Read people carefully and fine-tune your approach to meet *their* styles. People are drawn to others who remind them of themselves, even subtly. Don't misunderstand—I'm not suggesting that you be a phony. Instead, as my clients have shown me, we all have depth. Dig deep and transfer that element of your personality that connects with your listener's style. Otherwise, you risk being too direct, not direct enough, or missing the mark many other ways.

Give it the "Goldilocks Test"

- Not too hard
- Not too soft
- Make it just right

To reach a jokester, unlock your sense of humor. For a nit-picker, add relevant details. If you're dealing with someone who doesn't listen, use graphics and pictures to illustrate your points.

You'll also create chemistry by listening carefully and showing a genuine interest in others' needs and concerns. Lay out the benefits before launching into a data dump of factoids. Focus on your listener's needs and you'll both gain.

You'll also get faster, more positive connections by plugging into the right port. Ask your targets how they prefer to communicate when you can't meet face-to-face—by e-mail or phone calls? Use their favored method, not yours. Why leave voice-mails for people who prefer e-mail? Why waste time waiting for replies to e-mails that aren't opened promptly? Connect with your target's favored method and your results will soar.

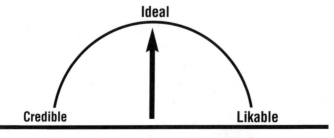

Where do you rate on this scale?

2. Balance credibility and likability

Merge these two elements and you'll connect much more effectively. Likability is a critical factor in your success. You'll get promoted, demoted, hired and fired based on how likable you are. Credibility is equally important. It allows you to display your depth and take the risks necessary to earn respect in the workplace and the marketplace.

It's the people who are both liked and respected who truly connect and, as a result, are most successful in the workplace.

Perception becomes reality. There's a word on the street about all of us. It's in your best interest to know what the word is about you and self-correct to enhance others' perceptions. Ask a trusted mentor or coach for 360° feedback. Aim to merge credibility and likability—and people will naturally be drawn to you and do what you ask.

3. Shoot straight

Shoot straight with absolute clarity. State your viewpoint clearly and directly. If there's any ambiguity in what you're saying, your listener's natural reaction may assign it the worst possible interpretation. Don't hide your agenda. Take a clear, unmistakable stand to let people know politely but precisely what you want them to do or think.

In my practice, I frequently see energetic, articulate professionals transform into bland vanilla when it's time to state their viewpoints or give presentations. Their energy levels plummet, their warmth disappears, their messages are garbled, and they dissolve into mind-numbingly robotic personas. Why does this happen to smart people? Fear.

Common Fears that Inhibit Straight Talk:

- Making a mistake
- Looking foolish in front of others
- Repelling people
- Hurting someone's feelings
- Feeling unqualified to speak up

Our fears cause us to play it *too safe* and homogenize ourselves—and our messages—as insurance policies against our fears. Big mistake.

Communication camouflage, as I call it, sucks the life right out of you. Wimping out and playing it too safe makes you predictable, boring, and unclear. You might as well slap a giant sticker on your forehead that says, "Change the channel!" If you homogenize yourself, people will be compelled to tune you out pronto—their grocery lists will be more riveting. I'm not proposing that you morph into Richard Simmons. Just don't conceal your natural warmth, energy, and clarity for your subject matter, or you'll miss connecting with your audience.

Step 2: Convey

Now that you've connected with your listener, aim to convey facts that build on that buy-in. This step is fact-based. If you aim properly with compelling, relevant content, you'll be succinct, stay on track, and boost recall. Many people make the costly mistake of attempting to deliver this step first—they jump in head-first and start conveying facts before they earn emotional buy-in. Emotions sell. Facts tell. Here are some tips to convey messages to build your case:

1. Talk in Triplets

Mental messages are best delivered in threes. The rationale behind this is a formula known as the "Trilogy of Persuasion" which dates back to the eighth century. People instinctively welcome information conveyed in threes.

The mental power of three:
- Red, white, and blue
- Lights, camera, action
- Ready, aim, fire
- Stop, look, and listen
- Earth, wind, and fire
- Knife, fork, and spoon

It's no coincidence these phrases share a common math. The mind is programmed to receive, store, and recall information presented in threes. (Did you notice that information was just offered in threes?) Give birth to triplets.

Deliver three targeted messages whenever possible. Think narrow and deep, not shallow and wide. Construct the messages to target the *listener's interests*, not yours. Do your homework. Discover their hot-button issues and build your key messages around these. Add additional triggers, also known as sub-points, as time permits.

Using this methodology serves to anticipate and bring forward any conflicts and deal-breaker issues. You'll draw differences to the surface (and the behind-the back complaining and assumptions that often accompany them) and take a giant step towards resolving issues, building buy-in, and triggering positive responses.

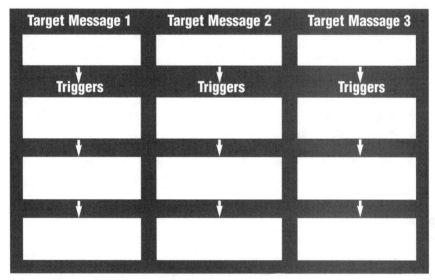

2. Plant visual nuggets

The eyes trump the ears. Always have, always will. Remember show-and-tell in kindergarten? What part of the equation sparked your interest—show or tell? Of course, it was the show portion. Photographs, charts, and other visuals build and reinforce your points. Pictures are powerful—for example, the images of prisoner abuse at Abu Ghraib in Iraq illuminated the issue far more effectively than any words ever could.

So what do you do if you don't have visuals to share? Use *action verbs* to plant visual software in your listener's mind. It's as close as you can get to programming their thoughts.

The benefit of planting visual nuggets is to help express complex ideas in bite-sized pieces. Mental pictures trigger accurate recall; the human mind is like a private screening room. Help people remember what you convey by adding visual words. Punch up your sentences. Use an active voice. Use clearer, shorter, more visual words. Here are some examples:

Instead of this:	Try this:
The concept is getting attention	The concept is snowballing
Sales are going up fast	Sales are skyrocketing
They're interested in our proposal	Our proposal piqued their interest
They're not talking about it now	Their lips are sealed

You don't have to exaggerate; just think visually. Use a thesaurus to transform boring words into more colorful language. Media commercials and sound bites are built around this principle. Talking—and thinking—in visual nuggets fine-tunes your messages and produces results.

3. Front-load your messages

Edit yourself or others will edit you. My clients report that they don't like the results when their listeners mentally edit them. Their listeners' interpretation of what's important doesn't correlate with their version of what's significant.

To avoid being edited, ask yourself, "What's the most important take-away point?" Front-load your messages with this point. People are more compelled to stay tuned in if you pique their interest early on. Frontloading serves two important purposes: 1) It helps you stay on track; and 2) it encourages your listener to stay tuned in.

Backloaded Message:

"You know, I've been talking to people about this cash flow problem we've been struggling with the last two quarters. Come to think of it, it was probably more than two quarters—I think it's actually three. Anyway, I've been trying to figure out an answer and I've come up with an idea. I'm not saying this is the best idea—I'm sure a lot of other people have ideas, too. Anyway, here's my thought…"

Frontloaded Message:

"I have a proposal to solve our cash flow issue. I believe we should..."

So get to the point quickly—frontload and trim your words to double your impact. Don't bury the good stuff. The days of "I'll save the best for last" are long-gone. Spilling everything you know at one time is unnecessary; if people want to know more, they'll ask and you can dig deeper.

Step 3: Convince

The final step allows you to hit the bulls-eye. Surprisingly, many of us fail to fire. Participants in my workshops and private coaching programs tell me they're afraid of being perceived as pushy or overly aggressive. But if you fail to finish a game, you automatically lose. Here are some techniques to help you be more persuasive:

1. Boost your energy level

Passion breeds energy. If you're not passionate about your subject, go back to the drawing board. Research it more thoroughly until you find an angle that lights a fire under you. Once you've developed that personal enthusiasm, let it show.

Here's a shortcut to instantly sound more convincing; rehearse your presentation into a tape recorder. When you replay the recording, you may be amazed at how dull and detached you sound. If you fall short of persuading yourself, it's highly unlikely you'll convince anyone else.

Checklist to self-correct with a tape recorder

- Listen to your first recording with your "script" in front of you.
- Highlight key words.
- Delete unnecessary words to tighten the message.
- Is your message clear and unambiguous?
- Did you miss any important points?
- Re-record.
- You'll sound much more persuasive and influential.

My clients experience identical reactions when they first hear their voices on tape. "That doesn't sound like me!" they say. Surprisingly, it does. The recorded voice is far more accurate than you think. Your head is filled with structures that reverberate when you talk. This anatomy creates the illusion (inside your head) that you're speaking more convincingly and energetically than you actually are. We all need to adjust our energy levels once we discover the true sound of our voices

2. Make your reasoning visible

If you meet resistance, it's often because people make assumptions based on what they *don't hear*. In the absence of facts, presumptions rule. These flawed assumptions drive negative behavior. Especially when change is involved, your listeners may feel that you're withholding information to keep them in the dark—which causes them to tune you out, or even worse, to fuel the rumor mill.

To counter these reactions, briefly reveal the reasoning behind significant decisions and viewpoints. Let your listener know the thinking that went into your decisions. You'll slash resistance and make it easier for people to buy into your ideas.

How to make your reasoning visible:

"These were the deciding factors..."

"Here's why I think this is the best way to go..."

To extract the reasoning from someone else:

"Can you help me understand your thinking here?"

"Could you walk me through the reasoning on that?"

When attempting to convince people to change their behaviors, be specific and outcome-oriented rather than generic.

Instead of this:

I want you to be more communicative.

Try this:

Please respond to my e-mails within an hour whenever possible.

3. Pull the Trigger

Short of a miracle, the only way to hit the bull's eye is to aim directly for it. Expect to do well and you'll command attention. Look and sound decisive—even if you don't feel confident inside. End your sentences with declarative inflection, and don't tag your sentences with verbal question marks that sound as if you need approval.

Coaching corporate leaders, I've found the primary reason that leaders fail to pull the trigger is perfectionism. My advice: resist the inner voice that says you're not fully prepared. Use the 80% rule: Communicate and get the ball rolling when you're 80% ready.

To gain authority when you pull the trigger, add power pauses. Pauses are a potent but underused tool to persuade. Pauses convey thoughtfulness and pique curiosity. Try this: fall silent, add direct eye contact, and see what happens. You'll generate interest. People will stop multi-tasking and give you their undivided attention. A power pause convinces listeners that you're both confident and competent.

Power pause technique:

- Pause before delivering a significant statement.
- Stop moving.
- Don't look away during the pause—make direct eye contact.
- Make your point.
- Add another pause after making the statement to let it sink in.
- Pause before answering a question.
- Count to three before replying.
- Ask yourself, "What's the main point the listener wants addressed?"

Remember the call to action—what are you trying to convince them to do or think? Don't be ambiguous. Be crystal clear. If you don't ask for anything, you'll get exactly what you asked for. Nothing.

Connect. Convey. Convince.™

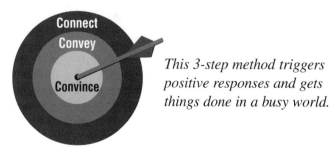

This 3-step method triggers positive responses and gets things done in a busy world.

When I left daily broadcasting to coach corporate leaders, many executives wanted to know if I could train them to be more charismatic. They thought this surface skill would help them become more influential.

Instead, I seek to offer something far more powerful. The three-step Target Talk™ methodology guides leaders to generate compelling, well-constructed content that cuts through clutter, triggers buy-in, and produces positive responses. Follow the process from start to finish and you'll tap into a uniquely powerful formula. You'll earn people's attention and gain positive results in today's increasingly inattentive workplace and marketplace.

Now...is that your belt loop ringing? Or mine?

ABOUT CONNIE DIEKEN

*C*onnie Dieken has an uncanny ability to communicate like a pro. She won a national public speaking championship—despite the fact that she had never delivered a speech before! For more than twenty years as a television news anchorwoman, talk show host, Emmy© award-winning reporter, and Telly© award-winning voice talent, Connie has been one of the country's most respected journalists and one of the few women inducted into the Radio & Television Broadcasters Hall of Fame.

She is now the president of Communicate Like a Pro™, a center for professional development which she founded in 2000. Based on her extensive experiences, Connie uses her innovative methodology to transform leaders into focused communicators. She helps people trigger positive responses and get things done through smart communication. Her unique approach guides leaders to master the dynamics of today's challenges to cut through communication clutter and generate buy-in.

A consummate professional, Ms. Dieken is an adjunct professor of communication skills at Corporate College in Cleveland, Ohio and has developed communication courses and strategic communication plans for corporations of all sizes. A graduate of Indiana University, she has authored dozens of communication articles appearing in publications nationwide, written communication workbooks, and recorded videos, CDs and DVDs. She is the founder of the trailblazing Target Talk™ and Message Maker™ systems.

Contact Information:
Connie Dieken
Founder & President
Communicate Like a Pro, LLC
Phone: 440-930-8500
Fax: 440-930-7555
E-mail: connie@communicatelikeapro.com
Website: www.communicatelikeapro.com

CAN YOU HEAR ME? REALLY?

by Michelle M. Weil, Ph.D.
& Christopher A. Weil

What you are about to encounter is a very special chapter. What you are about to read will give you information on making your communication clearer and helping you become more credible. This information will not only add to your confidence but the confidence of others listening to you, causing them to take you more seriously. Additionally, you will learn what goes wrong in communication, how to be more easily "heard," and how to really listen.

Sounds great, right? You bet!

Christopher, my brilliant deaf son, is my co-author for this chapter, We have written and been published together before, and who better than Chris to tell you about communication from the viewpoint of one not blessed with the ability to hear since birth, who has worked hard to become the outstanding scholar that he is today. Both Christopher and I tell it like it is, with no holds barred—clear, direct and confident communication.

Of course you (like everyone else) have no time to spare, but if I were you, I would make the time to read this chapter. It is brief, entertaining enough to keep you awake, and my guess is you will come away wanting to read it again and again. If you get really enthusiastic, you can read my two earlier book chapters, listed at the end of this one, where I tell you how to find more time. Everything I have ever written and said really can be done!

"Anyone who stops learning is old, whether at twenty or eighty. Anyone who keeps learning stays young.
The greatest thing in life is to keep your mind young."
—Henry Ford

So here we go, and let's get to it! Read on!

Here are some of the behaviors which occasionally keep us from communicating with excellence.

Old Unrecognized Patterns. Each of us formed patterns of communication early in life, either from what we heard or saw, or from those behaviors (or lack thereof) for which we received praise or rewards. For some, this may have been silence at home and not asking questions in school. In other words, being invisible. For others, it may have been to "speak your mind" whenever and wherever possible.

Whatever your early communication learning patterns may have been, if they are unhealthy, and you haven't worked on changing these patterns, they are still with you. Many of these tendencies may be unrecognized and yet still utilized. The unhealthy patterns have not only lost their usefulness but may cause major relationship, communication, and intimacy difficulties.

The irony is that, since many of us are totally unaware of our faulty communication patterns, we may be quite confused by the outcome of our conversations or other communications "that just don't seem to go right." We may say "yes" when our insides are saying "no" and do things for others to keep them happy. The list of possibilities is endless, so I shall just ask you to think about it.

Making Threats and Promises. Remember the old adage: "Actions speak louder than words"? Today this could not be truer. Many among us threaten, promise, apologize, cry fake tears, humble ourselves, beg forgiveness, and more, but do not change the underlying faulty behavior patterns. Without this behavior change—so that our words and actions match—we cannot truly be authentic or successful in our communication. In addition, our style cuts across everything, including, but not limited to, our friendships as well as our business and intimate relationships.

Truth be told, many of us feel empty inside. We try to fill the space with alcohol, food, legal and illegal drugs, cigarettes, relationship after relationship, overuse of technology, and so on. Too many of us keep our needs, feelings, wants, and desires to ourselves. We may think that "the right person" who truly loved us would just magically know these things and deliver the goodies we so clearly desire. Additionally, there are those of us who simply tell the wrong person and still get no goodies.

Others speak their minds without any consideration of the effect on those around them. These folks don't pause to reflect about the timing, place or potential outcome. They literally "barf" their mind whenever, wherever, and on whomever they wish. Have you ever been a barf recipient, literally or figuratively?

Not fun, is it?

I'll bet you can start to see why none of these work well!

One way to change these unproductive behaviors is through *compassionate communication*. Here we speak and listen with both our head and our hearts. What is this quality we call compassion? Compassion is a sympathetic feeling. It involves the willingness to put yourself in another person's situation, thereby taking the focus off yourself and imagining what the other is actually feeling. It is the recognition that others have problems, pain and frustrations, which are every bit as real as yours, and sometimes much, much worse.

Developing compassion takes practice, and it involves your personal commitment, intention, and action. You can't become a compassionate communicator until you develop your own personal compassion. Nothing contributes to our becoming a compassionate listener better than this sage advice: "Say what you mean, mean what you say —just don't say it mean."

Now don't give up! 'Tis not that tough—even for "tough" guys!

Here are a few more habits that get in the way of excellent communication.

The Fatigue Factor. Most of us are clueless about just how chronically fatigued we are, and have been for quite some time. A few of the signs we may show are that we can't spell as well as we used to, our handwriting is poorer than before, we rely on computers to type and spell check, and we don't remember clearly what we said or what was said to us.

The solution is multifaceted. First we must admit and accept this personal truth. Next, we typically need to re-prioritize our lives to make time for rest and relaxation. True R&R. We need more sleep, free time, "down time," whimsical time, time to muse and ponder, and time to be playfully impulsive in a way that serves our overall well-being.

Can I get your attention, please?

Ahhhh, multitasking now, aren't we? In previous books, articles and keynotes I (Dr. Weil) always discuss multitasking. In case you did not know, multitasking means doing more than one thing at the same time. In previous published works, I describe the term I have coined, "Multitasking Madness." As humans, we have the ability to multitask, but most of us have gone too far. Today, we are aided and abetted by technology.

We not only self-distract, but we cannot communicate with total accuracy when we multitask. As one of the leading experts on the subject, I unfortunately only see this behavior on the increase. For example, how many of you (now truthfully raise your hands) drive and talk on a cell phone at the same time? Or, what about (again, let's see those hands . . .) cooking, talking on the phone, and folding laundry while watching the boob tube?

Okay, relax those hands. Believe me, you are not alone.

Here's one of my personal strategies to improve my communication. My friends know that if I call on the phone (and I am blessed with exquisite hearing) and hear them typing or walking around on their mobile phone, I ask them one time to stop and focus on our conversation or what they will hear is the sound of a dial tone. This is a very important personal boundary for me. It is amazing how my friends, who have gone through my personal "training" program, now stop and talk with me. It also makes me feel important and loved—and they feel it too.

"Whether people are intimidated by technology or love technology—or are somewhere in the middle— they feel more stress because of Boundary Invasion and Multitasking Madness."

—Dr. Michelle M. Weil,
Workforce Magazine

Unfortunately, I (Chris Weil) have to deal with the opposite. In phone conversations with people, I must use CRS (California Relay Service), a special service for the Deaf involving an operator who helps facilitate the conversation between a Deaf person and a hearing person. Of course, the conversation almost always goes much more slowly than a natural discussion, as the other person must wait until I have finished talking (I have very understandable speech) into the phone. Then while the other person talks, the operator transcribes the response onto a little screen onto my phone (often stopping them to ask about spelling), and then the other party signals that they're finished so that I may reply.

Often, many of my hearing friends become frustrated with this process, and try to keep their phone conversations with me short. This reaction is unfortunate because it deprives me of some of the fun parts of talking on the phone for hours, such as getting off on tangents, and forgetting entirely why I called in the first place. When I speak with people "live" after a phone conversation, I usually ask them how the conversation went and how the operator performed, and encourage them to speak up during the conversation if they become impatient or need to switch operators. I also ask that they let me know what's happening on their end.

This idea holds true for all forms of communication—let the person on the other side of the communication know where you are!

Only a few facets of a discussion can come over any line of communication, so it's essential for all involved to help each other understand as much as they can about what each is experiencing. Without this sharing, all we're hearing (or reading) are voices and words.

As we all know, there are many ways to communicate. Focused listening and communication use all the following, and then some. Here are a few of the essential tools in your communications tool box, which needs to be kept close at hand at all times for true success

Communication Tool Box

- Words
- Expressions
- Eye contact
- Gestures
- Restatement
- Reflection

In this section we have offered some "dos" and "don'ts" about having our communication truly heard. Now we look at what happens when you actually can't be heard.

When You Can't "Hear Me" ... REALLY!

In this section, I (Chris Weil) use the typical Deaf terminology to refer to either Deaf people or people with hearing. The word "Deaf" is always capitalized, and hearing people are simply referred to as "hearing." Do not think that I'm trying to slight anyone—just consider this a little insight into Deaf culture!

Despite being disadvantaged in one major way, the Deaf possess several advantages over hearing people in terms of communication. An expression exists in Deaf terminology, known as "Total Communication," referring to communication using all available means—hands, mouths, faces, eyes, bodies, and posture—all of it. For example, sign language is not simply the use of hand signs, although it might seem so to the uninformed observer. It involves all the aspects of communication listed above, and more.

On the other hand—no pun intended—in communication, hearing people often limit themselves to their ears and mouths. In this way, they lose many of the possible and incredibly important nuances of communication.

Additionally, the Deaf must make an effort to clearly receive whatever is being communicated to them, while those with hearing typically take it for granted. In short, only the Deaf must pay attention wholly to what is being told and "shown" to them. As a result, they may achieve a greater understanding of what is being communicated, while those with hearing might tend to miss things through inattention.

Also, surprisingly enough, while the Deaf are handicapped in their ability to hear, they often benefit in their other senses. They might have above-average eyesight, visual-motor perception, an acute sense of smell, and so on. Through these enhanced abilities, they can pick up certain cues that hearing people might miss.

In their conversing, Deaf people often tend to be blunt, and say exactly what they mean—it is part of the culture. The Deaf do not pussy-foot around a topic; they cut right to the heart of it. On the other hand, hearing people might spend fifteen minutes talking about nothing at all, while trying to get up the nerve to discuss the real reason for their meeting.

When Deaf people need to verify something, they never ask "Can you hear (see) me?" Rather, they often ask "Can you *understand* me?" Deaf people understand the one major point in communication—simply receiving the information from one sense or another is not enough. All that does is send certain electrical impulses to your brain! To communicate, you must not hear or see, you must *listen and understand.*

Deaf people also encounter many barriers to communication that must be overcome to achieve the goal of total understanding. From the moment of discovery by the parents that their child is deaf, a vicious battle often ensues. The first major decisions to be made are how to raise the child in terms of language, physical development, and strategy. For the child's language, the decision falls anywhere between the extremes of teaching them sign language only, giving them an entirely oral education (no sign language), or finding some sort of compromise solution in between. It is a constant struggle for communication from day one, and it only gets worse. Options for the child's physical development range from getting a cochlear implant (involving brain surgery to attempt to "fix" the child's hearing), getting hearing aids, or none of the above. For the child's education, the parents must decide between main-streaming their child in normal hearing classes, putting the child in special deaf-only classes, or some combination of these.

Families can be unsupportive, for example, by declining to learn sign language or accommodate the Deaf child's unique needs. School systems can often be unreliable, by not providing enough services to meet the needs of the Deaf student or providing them inconsistently. Advocacy services are often lacking or confused, and the child receives so many conflicting messages from different sources that his or her entire life becomes a whirlpool of madness. Some children become rebellious and refuse to wear their hearing aids, or refuse to take speech therapy, or so on.

Even with all these things dragging Deaf people down, many still become great communicators, using the skills that their unique heritage gives them. For example, most people do not realize that the great composer Ludwig Van Beethoven actually became quite deaf in his later life and continued to compose great masterpieces. More recently, the Deaf actress Marlee Matlin, known for her Academy Award-winning performance in the film *Children of a Lesser God* has also enjoyed a good degree of success. Those connected with Deaf also tend to develop above-average communication skills from greater exposure to Deaf society. With its emphasis on understanding over sensing, the Deaf society teaches many people what the world needs to learn—to see, think, and understand.

What's All That Noise?

In today's world, there is so much racket! We are constantly bombarded by white noise, background noise, the noise played while we are on hold or in elevators. We are exposed and overexposed to televisions, radios, horn honks and more. Additionally, all of our technology fills our senses with beeps, buzzes and even the low-level hums of our computer hard drives at work.

Our self-talk is another form of noise. As we rehearse a conversation we will have, do a postmortem on one we did have, and ponder what someone should have done or said, we are filling our brains with racket. Our critical self, that voice that tells us where we blew it and so many other self-created forms of internal noise, bombards us from within.

With all this inner and outer distraction, excellent communication is all the more challenging. Here are some additional tips to help with the noise.

Tips for Hearing Yourself and Being Heard above the Noise

- Discover your passion, your authentic self.
- From the above, create a clear and focused work and life plan that suits you.
- Prioritize your life and work plan—making certain it includes your passion.
- Create a vision statement based on outcomes that are clearly measurable.
- Based on your above vision statement, define and target your market as needed.
- If you are marketing something, learn to tell others what you do, sell, or what your vision is, in one sentence.
- Use your talents, gifts and abilities to serve others—this helps you stay focused and sleep at night!
- Follow all of the above without fail.

> *"Knowing is not enough, we must apply.*
> *Willing is not enough, we must do."*

—Johann von Goethe

Never in our history has there been a greater need to become hearty in our spirit, solid in our actions, kind and gentle in our attitudes, and do whatever it takes!

ABOUT MICHELLE M. WEIL, PH.D.

*D*r. *Michelle Weil is an author, professional keynote speaker, corporate consultant, clinical psychologist, the "Miss Manners of Technology."* Published by John Wiley and Sons are her books TechnoStress: Coping With Technology @Work @Home @Play *which teaches you how to thrive in the age of high-tech, and* The Mental Health Technology Bible. *She wrote a chapter entitled: "Designing Boundaries at Work, Home and Play" in the book,* Maintain Balance in an Unsteady World. *She wrote a chapter entitled: "Stay the Driver . . . Not the Driven" in the book,* Work Smarter, Not Harder. *From* Good Morning America *to the* Wall Street Journal, *she is sought after for her commentary on resolving the stress that is created in our lives and by our lifestyles.*

Dr. Weil is a consistent contributor in professional and popular journals and magazines. She was recently featured by the San Diego Tribune *and authored "Rx for TechnoStress" in* Professional Speaker Magazine *(May 2003), published the article entitled "Stop, Breathe and Think . . . It's Time," in the* National Psychologist *(July/August, 2003), and was honored by being asked to be the closing keynote at the prestigious Terrorism 2004: The American Community Preparedness Conference.*

Through extensive media coverage including her roles as National Spokesperson for MCI, Activision and others; Dr. Weil has reached millions with her message and her wisdom. She heads the consulting firm Human-Ware, LLC, www.human-ware.com, is an avid speaker, trainer and writer, maintains a private clinical psychology practice, and is the proud mother of two brilliant teenagers (yikes!), one of whom is her co-author for this chapter.

ABOUT CHRISTOPHER A. WEIL

Christopher was born with a profound hearing impairment. He was fitted with hearing aids. He and his parents learned SEE sign language, and he started speech therapy, which he still continues. Currently 16 years old, he receives a fully mainstreamed education with full-time interpreters, and is a high school honors student with a 4.67 GPA. He is active in several high school clubs, including Key Club (a community service club), The Alliance for Acceptance and Open-Mindedness, Lancer Express (school monthly newspaper), and much more! He is fluent in ASL (American Sign Language) and has been instrumental in running four "standing room only" ASL Performances in his community. He spends his spare time in such activities as reading mysteries and science fiction, surfing the Internet, and playing video games. He is always looking forward to the future, and will be college-bound within a year. Destination? Unknown. Prospects? Great! Attitude? Excellent!

Contact Information
Michelle M. Weil, Ph.D.
Human-Ware, LLC
Phone: (760) 730-3894
E-mail: Weil@Human-Ware.com
Website: www.Human-Ware.com

LISTENING:
Create Profitable Results
with Clear & Compelling Communication

by Natalie R. Manor

It can be very clear when someone is not listening to us. And it can be very clear when we are not listening to others. And when we do not listen, we create a multitude of mishaps that start with being impolite and can extend to producing the wrong product.

Because I am an expert in leadership and communication, working with emerging leaders in executive development, people often tell me that their organization lacks good communication. The bedrock of great communication is listening. Listening means to make a conscious effort to hear.

Effective listening is hearing the information, comprehending the information given and taking action, asking questions, or responding to what we have heard. Effective listening is also a way of listening with attention, respect, and the whole body.

In the world of presentation skills training, there are common statistics that each trainee is taught. They are:

55% of communicating is through body language

38% of communicating is tone of voice and pacing

7% of communicating is the written word

These statistics hold true for people throughout the world. We communicate most powerfully, first through our body; secondly, with our voice, and thirdly, with the written word.

Our body language shouts to those we are with. Picture someone sitting in a chair, arms crossed and turned to the side looking at the ceiling. How interested do you think they are in what is being said? Probably not at all.

Picture someone sitting in a chair, leaning forward toward the speaker, smiling and writing down notes of everything he or she is hearing.

Use those same examples and add speaking to them. The person who is sitting in a chair, arms crossed, and looking at the ceiling and speaking in a tight, monotonous voice is indicating displeasure with the conversation or situation.

The person who is sitting in the chair and leaning forward with a big smile is responding in an animated way, indicating he or she is enjoying the situation and can't wait to get more of it.

If I were the person presenting or speaking, I would choose the big smile over the crossed arms each time.

The examples may be extreme, concerning what is good listening and what is not, but these are not unusual occurrences in business. Many of the issues that contribute to difficult or poor communication within an organization are directly related to people not listening or giving the impression they are not listening.

As I work with emerging leaders within the executive teams in organizations, I find that reeducating people on what good listening is clears up many of the communication problems.

When people are listened to, they feel valued. When people feel valued, they work more effectively and create sustainable and valuable results for themselves and their organizations.

Who Needs To Listen

A popular game with children is called "Telephone". You form a line and someone tells the first person in line a piece of information. That person tells the next person and then the next person and the next, until the last person in line hears what is being said. The last person in line is then supposed to say out loud to the group what he heard.

This game can produce peals of giggles for the group because the last person usually says something that is *nothing* like the original piece of information.

And I find this "game" is in full play within organizations, large and small.

Several aspects of not listening contribute to the issue of information being mis-spoken and mis-heard. The most common aspects of not listening well (or not at all) fall into the following categories:

1. Who taught you to listen?

2. Gender—male and female

3. Judgment

4. Time—doing more with less

5. E-mail

6. Interruptions

1. Who taught you to listen? Think back for a moment about your most significant teacher when you were young. Was it your mother, school teacher, priest, aunt, brother? And what kind of communicator were those people? Were they effective, thorough, good listeners, and do you really want to be like them as listeners?

Our earliest lessons sometimes are our deepest lessons. We keep these lessons for our entire life and many times do not think much about them. But if these early teachers, however much we love and respect them, were not good communicators and listeners, it might be worthwhile to see how much of them is still left in our listening behavior.

2. Gender—male and female communication. There have been dozens of books written about how men and women communicate, or don't. One of the most widely read of these is *Men are from Mars and Women are from Venus*, by John Grey. When his book first came out it was the first popular venue for men and women to openly acknowledge that the way we communicate is different.

For the most part, women tend to be relationship oriented and men appear to be strategic or solution oriented. We also have discovered that our brains are wired differently, which accounts for the difference in communication and behavior.

Men and women speak differently, ask questions differently, compile reports differently, and deal with customers differently. Unless

there is an understanding that each way of communicating in these situations has advantages, then the outcome can be negative.

Women bring interpersonal language to the work place. Men bring
the language of planning and goals. When these gender abilities are recognized and used to the organization's advantage, they can prove to be
very profitable and valuable.

Women tend to need more time to speak and require active body
language responses so they know they have been heard. They also appreciate immediate feedback on what has been said or presented. They tend
to make their stories longer and to include personal information.

Men tend to speak more in stats and numbers and need less body
response to know they have been heard. Men tend to need less
feedback and language. They tend to need longer mulling or decision
time. Men also "hear" better when dealing with only two or three
pieces of information at a time.

3. Judgment. In my experience in dealing with leaders and teams,
judgment seems to be the most damaging aspect of communication
issues. It occurs when we begin listening to someone, assume we know
what he or she is saying, and what he or she will be saying, and judge the
value of the communication even before the person finishes speaking.

The act of judging while listening can have less influence if you are
aware of the fact that you are doing it. You might even be doing it now
while you are reading these words. Making the assumption that you
know what I am going to say before it is even presented on this page
limits your learning.

The act of judging while people are speaking can limit your professional growth. Not only are you not hearing what people are saying,
you are not getting the value of the information they are presenting. If
you miss the information, you limit your creativity, thought process,
ability to contribute to what is being offered, and you stay in your
judgment mode.

Judgment is often prevalent when you are listening to people with
different accents, different opinions from your own, or new ways of presenting information. When you are thinking instead of listening, you are

not allowing yourself to absorb new information. Whether the information is different from what you know, or maybe not even correct, when you listen you gain clarity and support creativity in being able to add to the information being presented.

4. Time—doing more with less. In my opinion, the speed of our doing business is the biggest contributor to less effective communication. I find it odd that with all the new ways of communicating, our skills are less honed and our impact is impaired. The lack of time is not an excuse to not listen and communicate well. If you do not have time to converse or to listen well, let the person know and pick a better time for the conversation. People can be very offended if you are standing in the hallway, tapping your foot, and moving in another direction while they are sharing important information with you. Plus, your listening in that situation is probably flawed: you did not take notes, you were thinking about other issues and felt rushed, and you did not have a good rapport with the speaker.

You can slow down. You can listen. You will be much more productive when you examine your listening habits and begin to modify them for yourself and the others that need you to listen to them.

5. E-mail. While most of us would not be able to survive without the use of e-mail in our daily lives, we are also drowning in it. Many of the executives I work with receive 250 to 350 e-mails a day. Most e-mail consists of replies to replies of e-mails, do not set context, are sent to more people than they need to go to, are not easily read, and contain the most egregious spelling and grammar errors because we are working so quickly.

Some tips for writing a good e-mail:
- Make sure the subject line refers to the body of the message. Change the subject line if the message changes so you can file it and easily retrieve it.
- *Do not* make your paragraphs longer than 3-4 lines. Reading dense e-mails with no paragraph breaks is almost impossible, key points may be missed, and the human eye does not read well with a mass of information in its view.

- When you are confirming a meeting or time, a time to speak or information you are sharing, set the context in the opening line with: "So we are meeting at 2:00 pm on 7/3 at Jason's Tavern in London." This will be helpful for you and the other people as you won't have to search the entire e-mail for the information, and you will clearly state what you have agreed to. I've received countless "thank you's" from people telling me that my restating what we agreed to was very helpful.
- Send your e-mails only to people who need the information.
- Try not to use bcc. It does not create a feeling of trust within the others receiving the e-mail if they do not know who else is receiving it.
- Make e-mails concise and to the point. People will appreciate that you save them time and will want to read your e-mails.
- Use people's names and sign your name to e-mail. "Hi, Bob, Hello Sue." "Thanks from Natalie." This technique personalizes the e-mail and it confirms that you are paying attention to the relationship. Everyone likes to see his or her name used.

6. Interruptions. The frantic pace of our days creates the need to get information *now*. We are interrupted by the telephone, people stopping in, e-mail, pagers, and cell phones. Our technology has created a pace of communicating that creates much miscommunication but little support for listening.

Here are a few suggestions for clearing up the communication pipeline in order to listen in a proactive and positive way:

1. Stop what you are doing when someone comes to speak with you. Look at the speaker, turn your chair to him or her, stop typing, and show your interest through your body language. If you do not have time to listen, set up another time that will work, but use positive body language and tone of voice when speaking.
2. If you answer the telephone and are still typing on your keyboard, you are not listening. Either stop the typing or let voicemail take the message. Listening requires full attention and

an awareness of the information being spoken or presented.

3. Let people know that you are going to have quiet time during the day and post the times so others will know that you are not available to them. However, when you are available, use all the techniques of good listening so people will feel valued and you will get the information you need.

What Great Listening Skills Get You

When people feel listened to, they feel as if they have earned your respect and trust. These are some of the top characteristics that my seminar attendees name as important in high-value relationships. When people feel respected and trusted, they do good work.

Effective communication within an organization is directly tied to higher productivity and profits. Ineffective listening causes errors, whether in the engineering department, sales and marketing, distribution, or elsewhere. Wrong information—information not heard or listened to creates wrong outcomes.

People who are good listeners are good communicators. They are liked, trusted, and known for doing good and creative work. People who are good communicators are given high-profile projects to complete because people know they will do good work. People who listen well carry out work well.

There are no long-term, consistently excellent leaders who do not listen and communicate well. It is not possible to run an organization effectively without listening to what the employees need, what the customers want, and what the marketplace is saying.

What Listening Gives to Others

- A sense that you care about what is being said
- Better service
- Confidence, trust, and respect
- Appreciation of their efforts
- An excellent product, service, and relationship
- Trust in dealing with you

What Value Listening Provides

- Profits—through assurances that information will be understood the first time and tasks will be completed correctly
- Speed and ease in doing business
- Excellent products and services
- Referrals and repeat business
- Total confidence in the process

You are more than welcome to take the listening test on my web site, www.NatalieManor.com. It has 26 questions that will give you a good overall indication of your listening skills. A grade will be provided at the end and sent to you with comments on where you might like to improve.

Listening Test Examples from my Web Site

The following six questions in the listening test provide some useful information about how you listen. You can take the test now with these questions. To the left of each question, rate yourself on a scale of 1 (low rating) to 5 (high rating) on each of the following statements:

___1. I seldom have difficulty waiting until someone finishes talking so I can have my say.

___2. I listen even when I do not particularly like the person who is talking.

___3. I put away what I am doing while someone is talking with me.

___4. I withhold all judgment and opinions until I have heard all a person has to say.

___5. I respect a person's right to his or her opinions, even if I disagree.

___6. I view most disputes or conflicts as an opportunity to understand the person better.

Results: If you got a 30, you are a wonderful listener. If you received a score of 20–26, you are a good listener, but sometimes lose interest. If you received a score of less than 20, you probably need to take a good look at your listening skills.

If you did not do well on these six questions, it is a wake up call that you might behave according to some of the non-listening patterns we discussed earlier. I find the best way to find out if I am a good listener is to ask the following questions.

1. Do you feel listened to when we communicate with each other?
2. What would you change about my listening style?
3. What is the number one indicator you get from me that I am not listening?
4. What is the number one indicator you get from me that I am listening?
5. Is my non-listening only with you or have you observed it when I communicate with others?

You might want to give yourself a way of testing your new way of listening by doing a two-week trial period of listening in a way that others actually know you are listening. Tell people you are working on your listening skills so they can help you know what's working and what's not.

To be listened to is a gift . . .

Excellent communication begins with listening. Bottom line profits, measurable results and high-value performance are all the result of good communication. But it will not happen without good listening.

Strategies for Success[SM] Best Practices for Listening:

- Show up for each one-on-one conversation as a great listener—use the body language
- Allow yourself to understand the other person before you give your opinion
- Silence produces profound listening
- Pick one new person each day to practice effective and profound listening with and keep track of the results
- Let people know you are working on your listening skills
- Give yourself space to learn this new skill well
- Look for feedback on how you are doing

Human relations—the building of a high-value relationship—has never changed. It does not matter how much we have to do, at what speed it needs to be done, and who is doing it, humans want and need to be listened to.

After all the surveys are done regarding what people want within an organization, it always boils down to "the desire to be appreciated and acknowledged." And being listened to tops the list of how appreciation can be shown.

I wish you good listening in all your communication.

ABOUT NATALIE R. MANOR

*N*atalie Manor works with emerging leaders to help them move from managing issues to leading people. She provides the means to develop extraordinary, high value relationships—both personally and professionally—in order to become superior performers. She is an executive coach, consultant, speaker and co-author of Magnetic Leadership, Wholehearted Success and Give Stress a Rest. She offers powerful, practical and on-target advice for mastering executive and team excellence, executive skill building and communication. Natalie also instructs on corporate workplace issues, with an emphasis on developing executive women.

Her KICKS audio tapes have been endorsed internationally in publications such as Entrepreneur, Self, Runners World, USA Today, Kiplinger's, Prevention, Men's Health, and Paul Harvey's Report. She has appeared on BBC's AllNight and on hundreds of radio and TV stations. Natalie stays current with memberships in the National Speakers Association, International Coaching Federation and American Society for Training and Development.

Contact Information:
Natalie R. Manor, CEO
Natalie Manor & Associates (NMA)
Northeast Headquarters:
P.O. Box 1508
Merrimack, NH 03054
Southeast Headquarters:
317 Hickory Bluff
Johnson City, TN 37601
Phone: 800-666-2230
E-mail: CoachNatalie@NatalieManor.com
Website: www.NatalieManor.com

COMMUNICATION
AND MANNERS

by Dana May Casperson

Y ou may think of communication as just the words you use. Really, the topic is more extensive than that. Communication entails all that you are, say, and do. Communication occurs through your body language, gestures, word choice, intonation, grammar and diction, the way you dress, your conversation topics, dining habits, table manners, jewelry, business accessories, cell phone use and e-mail correspondence, and all manner of other actions.

The greatest personal challenge is to coordinate every aspect of your communication to make all the elements consistent. This is a lifelong journey of refinement. Your credibility can be damaged or derailed when you pay no attention to these elements or think they just don't matter. Communication and leadership go hand in hand.

You probably know a brilliantly creative colleague who dresses like a slob, eats like a boar, talks like a boor, or tells offensive jokes. You probably choose not to be around that person unless it is necessary and only for short periods of time. Human nature keeps the negative in the forefront of your mind. First impressions are important, and bad encounters reinforce the image.

Everyone's personal challenge, then, is to work to polish any "rough edges" in one's professional presence. This presence can be divided into three areas of development: Visual, Verbal, and Virtual.

Visual is what people see. What people see is what they perceive you to be. This perception includes your wardrobe, gestures, and body language. We live in a visual-byte culture where we make judgments in two to four seconds. That first impression is lasting, and rarely do we have an opportunity to make another one. So, why not make the first impression superb?

Verbal is all that a person hears from you—your verbal communication and your voice messages.

Virtual is everything about you that does not include your presence or voice, such as your written communication on paper and on screen.

Look deeper at the three V's.

Visual

Your visual impression is what I call your visual resumé. What people see tells all about you, your respect for them, how you feel at that given moment or day, and how competent you are in the situation.

How to polish the rough edges is what Power Etiquette is all about. This is an ongoing learning process. Some skills change with the level of professional responsibility, and some behavior expectations change with the times. Each decade produces subtle changes in dress, communication, and methods of conducting our business. Always keep in mind that when change is needed, ask yourself if these changes are congruent with your value system and beliefs. As a leader, you guide the direction of the organization, association, group, or business. You set the tone for procedures and success. Never compromise solely for money. The decision to do so can easily be the ruin of the company.

Your wardrobe is an important part of your visual impression, so plan your clothing for optimum visual impact. You need to:

1. Plan your wardrobe like you make a business plan. Coordinate your wardrobe by color and style to include four trousers/skirts and pants (four total); four button-front and polo shirts, five ties/four blouses and sweaters; four jackets and sweater jackets. This combination can be maximized to more than forty different outfits.

I call this the "4 + 4 + 4 = 40 formula."

- Maximize every possible combination of clothing.

- Maintain your wardrobe.

- Update it each year with new color or style.

- Make certain the garments fit.
- Determine that the clothing is appropriate for your body type and work situation.

2. Check your body language. If it doesn't match your words, you sabotage your message.

- Do you stand tall?
- Do you drag your feet?
- Do you lean on walls and desks when you stand?

3. Your gestures should be appropriate for the situation and location. Eliminate distracting gestures like:

- Pushing up your glasses.
- Throwing your hair over your shoulder.
- Rubbing your earlobe.
- Sucking through your front teeth.
- Biting your nails.
- Chewing on hair.
- Twisting your mustache.
- Jangling coins and keys in trouser pockets.

4. The maintenance of your teeth, nails, hair, and clothing should be impeccable.

- Shoes should be polished and in good repair.
- Tattoos should be covered.
- Change hairstyle every few years.
- Hair should be secured back if it is longer than shoulder length.
- Nails should be clean and buffed.
- Make-up should be in moderation.

- Not more than two earrings on each side.
- Hems and cuffs should be intact and not frayed.
- Facial hair, if allowed, should be trimmed and shaped.

Verbal

One kind word can last a lifetime. You can make a difference through what you say or do not say. One sentence of well-chosen words can change the entire direction of someone's career. However, keep in mind that what you think you say may not be what someone else hears. The old adage "say what you mean and mean what you say" refers to the power of credibility and competence. If you say it, mean it and do it. Never promise to do something you have no intention of doing. Your words need to be well chosen, meaningful, and respectful. Avoid slang and swear words. Keep your industry lingo to office conversations; others may not know what you are talking about.

Your words must mirror your body language or you destroy your credibility. Slouchy posture and loud, rapid speaking are not congruent. Get in touch with your visual and verbal messages to align them for power.

All speaking is public speaking because whenever you speak, someone is listening. If your leadership position requires speaking more frequently or to large audiences, you might choose to work with a coach or join a Toastmasters® group to ease your fears and improve your speaking delivery. Remember that everyone can benefit from coaching to fine-tune his or her speaking style.

Your voice messages are part of your verbal resumé. The outgoing message should be energetic and informative. If you do not frequently change it, call yourself and check your outgoing message. Try changing it every month if you do not make a daily message change.

When you leave a voice message be certain that it includes:

1. Your name and phone number.
2. Your reason for calling.
3. Your message.
4. Your name and phone number.

By leaving your name and phone number at the beginning and end of the message, you help the listener get the number correctly, reinforce your name, and eliminate the need to listen again to the message. Make it easy for the person to return your call. Speak slowly and clearly. Speak the numbers as though you are writing each one.

Smile when you speak; it "sounds" in your voice. Phone calls and e-messages should be returned within 48 hours. Be a powerful communicator by choosing clear, concise words. Your power comes from being understood.

Virtual

Virtual communication is all that we say and do on paper and with words on a screen without intonation or explanation. Any time you put a pen to paper or fingers to keyboard you are displaying your professional skills. Spellchecker does not correct everything. When you are sending correspondence—especially contracts, proposals, and letters—print them out, stand, and read aloud. Reading out loud helps find the errors not seen by sight-reading. Lucky you, if you have staff to read your outgoing correspondence. Most of us must take editing responsibilities, which are vital for professional communication. Errors occur, so be lenient of others to a point; but your credibility is assessed and measured by the reader on every piece of written communication. Spelling is not all there is to writing; word choice and grammar, capitalization and punctuation are key elements to good writing.

Technology has made us available 24/7 or 12/5. There is ease in contacting people whenever and wherever they are. With that ability, we are faced with more challenges to respond. People make demands on our response time with their expectations of a quick answer. Technology such as e-mail, pagers, faxes, mobile phones, office phones, text messages on mobile phones, and instant messaging makes it possible to receive a higher volume of communication which, in turn, must be dealt with and managed in some way.

Instant messaging is rapidly becoming an office communication tool. Get ready for this technology because it will soon be part of many offices. IM, as it is called, is more intrusive than e-mail because a message box appears on the monitor screen. If several people are in IM communication with you, your screen could be covered with little boxes. IM software has not been perfected sufficiently for everyone's use, but indications are that IM will soon be commonplace in offices. Its use varies from customer service questions, to outside sales needing answers from the office, to interoffice communication with several people at once.

There is no end to the possibilities for virtual communication in the future. What we must determine is, how efficiently are we going to manage the demands? This decision takes conscious planning about how and when we are available and how rapidly we will respond.

Some people receive 200 e-mail messages daily. The reading and response time involved takes a significant amount of the workday and can undermine productivity.

Time management becomes the challenge for dealing with the demands made on your professional life. Leaders need to set the parameters for use, followed by discussion with staff on technology use in the office and employee rights for use of office software. These steps are crucial to productivity and competence. Credible communication means polishing the three V's of power to master the art of leading others to greater productivity.

Now that you understand how vital your choices are for professional power, consider the following seventeen power tips. Work on improving yourself because these make the difference between normal and extraordinary leadership.

Seventeen Tips to Develop Your
Professional Communication Style

1. Get a grip

Your handshake speaks loudly about your confidence and competence. There is a special sense of connection when you shake hands with someone. To make it magnetic, practice with someone you trust. Get comments from both men and women because men shake hands differently with women than with men. You want to:

- Position your feet so that you are facing the person.
- Look the person in the eye.
- Speak the person's name while shaking hands.
- Keep the hands vertical with thumb on top.
- Fit the hands web to web.
- Shake firmly, not softly.
- Shake three to seven seconds.
- Shake hands often.
- Smile.

2. Be prepared

Carry your papers and briefcase in your left hand, thereby keeping your right hand free and ready to shake hands. If you get in the habit of keeping your right hand free of papers when you are out and about, especially in networking situations, you will always be ready to shake hands.

3. Make introductions

Your ease with introductions makes people feel comfortable around new acquaintances and provides small information bytes so that a conversation can continue beyond the hellos. Think of an introduction as a circle. When introducing two people:

- Speak the name of the highest-ranking person first.
- Use first and last names.
- Speak the names twice as you "make the circle."
- Mention a small bit of information about each person, but not too personal.
- Look at each person as you make the introduction.

"Cyndi Novak, I would like to introduce (or like you to meet) Heather Andrade, our HR director. Ms. Andrade, this is Ms. Novak, Project Manager for ABC Corporation. Heather recently vacationed in Hawaii and I think you also like to vacation there, Cyndi." The two now have a common thread of interest on which to begin a conversation.

If you are not sure who is the higher-ranking person, make the introduction anyway. It is better to say the wrong name first than not make an introduction at all.

A self-introduction is a 10-second or less statement about yourself and what you do. If you write this out in advance to make it clear and concise, then you can practice it. You can give a lot of information in a short time. Mention your name (first and last), your position, and the benefits of your business or service.

"Hello, my name is Dana May Casperson. I have a dual first name. I am an author and speaker on Magnetic Leadership, the Power Etiquette skills that open doors money cannot. My company provides your ticket to professional success."

4. Dress for respect

Plan your wardrobe so that it is respectful to yourself and the others you work with. This means that your choice of attire should be appropriate for your industry, geography, culture, time of day, season, your body shape and personal style.

5. Deliver what you promise

Be realistic about what you will do. If you say that you will send the report or make a recommendation, do it. There is nothing more likely to discredit your credibility than to promise and not carry through. Your example for others serves as a model for them to do the same for you.

6. Answer it

Return e-mails and phone calls personally, if possible, as quickly as convenient and within 48 hours.

7. Acknowledge your co-workers

Do this every day.

- Use the magic words of "Please," "Thank you," "I'm sorry," "Excuse me," "Hello" and "Goodbye."

- Acknowledge your co-workers through words: "I appreciate your effort", "Can you help me finish this project?"

- Show that you value your co-workers.

- Demonstrate respect to your co-workers by your actions and words.

8. Listen

Learn to ask questions and to listen for the answers. You learn more than you can imagine by asking and listening. The staff that is doing the unrecognized work has insight and knowledge that others do not. Spend time with them in the employee lounge and ask for their observations and opinions. You may be surprised by their insights into the company.

9. Make conversation an art

When you are informed and interesting to talk with, people will be attracted to you.

Learn by:

- Reading and listening to the daily news.

- Reading weekly national news magazines.

- Knowing what is going on in your community.

- Being aware of what is happening in national sports.

- Going to the movies.

- Being able to recommend at least one current good movie.

- Knowing what books are on the best selling list.

- Reading outside your industry publications.

10. Use mobile phones thoughtfully

One quick way to polarize potential clients, clients or colleagues is to use your mobile while with them. Mobile phones are great tools of communication when used courteously. When in doubt, turn your mobile off. If you must take a call while with others, mention before the phone rings that you are expecting a call and ask if you may accept it. When the phone rings, get up and leave the room after you say "Hello," and before you begin the conversation.

Courteous mobile phone use includes:

- Turning it off during meetings (at meals, in offices, conferences, and home meetings).
- Turning it off during social events (concerts, plays, religious services, funerals and movies).
- Speaking softly when conversing.
- Not conducting job interviews, business deals, personnel issues.
- Moving to a quiet place away from others to converse.
- Choosing a non-intrusive ring tone.

11. Be a gracious host

Participate in the art of fine dining by learning how to use the dining tools while conversing. Your credibility shines brightly at the dining table when you know how to make people feel at ease. Know how to guide the conversation when it goes off course, select easy-to-eat items off the menu, handle the knife and fork correctly (illustration 1), recognize all the tableware, (see illustration 2), and know when to close the conversation.

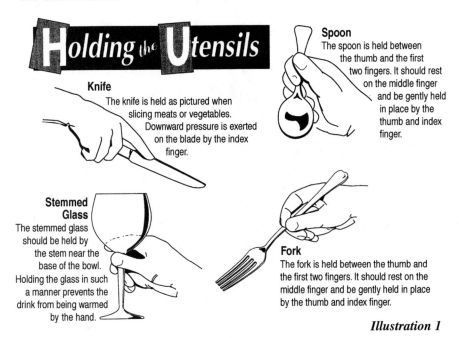

Holding the Utensils

Knife
The knife is held as pictured when slicing meats or vegetables. Downward pressure is exerted on the blade by the index finger.

Spoon
The spoon is held between the thumb and the first two fingers. It should rest on the middle finger and be gently held in place by the thumb and index finger.

Stemmed Glass
The stemmed glass should be held by the stem near the base of the bowl. Holding the glass in such a manner prevents the drink from being warmed by the hand.

Fork
The fork is held between the thumb and the first two fingers. It should rest on the middle finger and be gently held in place by the thumb and index finger.

Illustration 1

Illustration 2

12. Become an expert

Learn something well outside your profession. Develop an outside interest, which may involve community service, volunteering, or learning. To become magnetic and well educated, you need to study outside your industry. Of course, the study may be a lifetime of learning.

Possible topics could include ones you already have a special interest in:

- Foreign language
- Photography
- Old car restoration
- Painting

- Bicycling
- Travel
- Geography
- Winemaking
- Tea tasting
- Fishing
- Sailing
- Art

13. Get out of the rut

Know what is going on in your family, at their schools, and in the community. In order to stay up at the top of your profession, you need to know future as well as current industry trends.

Personally, you need small challenges to prod yourself to improve, refine, and grow. Make those small, incremental challenges to avoid being overwhelmed. Write your goals and purpose. Check them for completion at the end of six months. You will be pleased at the results.

I decided I needed to eat better and reduce my weight. My doctor and I spoke about it but his suggestion was to eat smaller portions. That was too vague for me. I joined Weight Watchers®, which taught me about better eating. The results? I have followed the plan rigidly and reached my desired goal.

14. Exercise

There is nothing that can substitute for good health. Exercise helps your body function well and makes you feel more alert and able to cope with work challenges. This has been one of the most difficult activities to put into my life. It has come and gone with the decades.

I do not like to exercise regularly at a gym. Recently, I found a way to increase my strength to tone my muscles, which works very well for me. I have a trainer through a program called Super-Slow® (SuperSlow.com). Twenty minutes once a week is "doable" for my lifestyle. The results are phenomenal. I have a stronger body, better posture, and feel healthier. Try some exercise and you will get results as long as you set short-term, reachable goals.

15. Hit the road

Travel opens the mind and helps us appreciate what we have. You may travel on weekends to local celebrations and events or plan annual or semi-annual trips to other countries. There is no doubt that traveling expands your interests and helps you to understand other ways to solve problems. For me, annual European bicycling trips expand my thinking, knowledge, and experience plus provide exercise.

16. Laugh a little

Develop a sense of humor to relieve the stress. It is always best to laugh at yourself and your mistakes. Never play tricks or tell jokes about others, especially co-workers and colleagues.

17. Smile

Smile often, even when you don't feel like it. Smiles are contagious and a smile relieves tension to make people feel more comfortable.

Communication is more than directing people to be more productive; it is about modeling behavior that is thoughtful, creative, sincere, credible, competent, and respectful. A powerful communicator provides a comfortable, caring environment in which others can express their concerns. When colleagues and co-workers feel valued and respected, they are more productive. The trickle down process works in even the shortest professional ladder. A leader who is thoughtful of others and values their expertise, inspires co-workers, in turn, to care about each other.

Polish the three "V's" for success; then challenge yourself to the power tips that polish your professional communication skills. Professional polish is a continual growth line. As we face new situations, we can weather them. We just need to have a foundation of respectful attitude toward others and ourselves. From there, we must keep learning and improving ourselves because in the process, we become better people to lead organizations and businesses. The magnetic field is created from the mix of talent and professional presence. You are a communication leader wherever you go.

Polish your professional image with power-Power Etiquette. Using clear communication through all the aspects of your being you create a magnetic field in which people are attracted to you. Your ability to communicate credibility and confidence helps those around you to be more productive. Keep an open mind, develop interesting conversation, an expanse of knowledge, and then wrap it in a pleasing way. Your power comes from being fascinating, honest, highly ethical and caring. Continue to learn and modify your thinking because Power Etiquette is the communication leadership skill that opens doors that money cannot.

ABOUT
DANA MAY CASPERSON

*D*ana May Casperson is the director of The Power Etiquette Group, a company which provides corporations, associations and clients with their ticket to professional success. She helps clients develop their business savvy for enhancing professional and client relationships. Dana May's audiences of all sizes have benefited from her expertise on "Seal the Deal at the Meal," "Moose on the Loose," "Threads of Success," "E-Talk: The New Rules, Power Protocol" and "The Art of Doing International Business." Dana May is an active member of National Speakers Association, California Society of Association Executives, her local Chamber of Commerce and Convention & Visitors Bureau, and is past president of the Sacramento chapter of the National Speakers Association, She is a nationally recognized Power Etiquette Expert who has delivered practical messages for Pacific Bell, the Ritz Carlton Hotels, the Fairmont Hotels, Edward Jones Financial, Allmerica Financial, Medtronics, Sola Optical USA, several universities and business associations.

Contact Information:
Dana May Casperson
The Power Etiquette Group
P.O. Box 3637
Santa Rosa, CA 95402
E-mail: danamay@PowerEtiquette.com
Website: www.PowerEtiquette.com

CONVERSATIONS WITH MYSELF

By Mark Christopher Drury

I began a remarkable transformation of body, mind, and character in October of 2000. I did not plan for it to happen. I was unaware of the real reason for its inception. The fruition of this change has been playing out for several years now.

This "thing" has turned into an amazing adventure.

I weighed 422 pounds on October 1, 2000. I am only 5'8" tall and have a medium frame. My life was miserable. Obesity and I were longtime companions. I had all the ailments that are associated with morbid obesity, such as diabetes, sleep apnea, swelling, depression, and chronic fatigue.

Many people think of the word "communication" and automatically imagine two or more people sharing words, messages, and thoughts. Those of us in business, marriages, and other relationships are constantly being reminded that improvements in our communication skills will make us better managers, spouses, and friends. We rarely think of communication as an internal skill that we can improve upon to help free ourselves from our inner demons and from situations that render us helpless. My transformation began to take root when I began to analyze my internal dialogue and to realize that I could micro-manage it to my advantage.

People often ask me, "Mark, what exactly was the straw that broke the camel's back? What made you finally decide that enough was enough?"

I have to reply that I really do not know. I was just sitting on the couch that Sunday in 2000 when I decided to jump up and join the Northeast YMCA in Louisville. The experience was just like the Stephen King novel, *Christine*: I got in the car and the car drove itself to the YMCA. I knew how to swim, so I planned to sneak in there before work around 6 a.m., put on my 5X swim trunks, and backstroke for thirty or so minutes without being noticed. My membership also entitled me to a mandatory weight-room introduction with a personal trainer. The trainer assigned to me, George McCoy, had lost 180 pounds in 1990. He saw a reflection of himself in me and "took me to raise." He threatened to kill me if I quit coming! He was determined to rescue me from my situation. I was determined to let him.

I was like a house on fire that first month. I lost thirty pounds in thirty days just exercising and eating properly. I bought Bill Phillips' *Body for Life* book and signed up for one of his twelve-week challenges. I began getting compliments from everyone at work, at home, and at church. My spirits were soaring. I began to notice physical changes. My pants were falling off me. You could actually see that I had a neck. I became one with the treadmill and the elliptical trainer. I think my professional speaking career was in its infancy during the latter part of that first year. If anyone got within three feet of me, my mouth opened, and I began talking about my transformation in progress. I lost an unbelievable ninety pounds that first year.

What was so different this time? I had been on every weight loss plan in the world, yet I had failed miserably for twenty-five years to slay this demon. From 1995 until 2000, I had not even attempted to lose weight again. I told myself that this particular ship had already sailed. I told myself that never again would I put myself in the situation of thinking that I could ever escape from this stranglehold that obesity had on me. I told myself that this as just my destiny, my cross to bear in life. I told myself that if I was ever to achieve any level of happiness in my life, I would just have to accept my plight and make peace with it. I was a fat guy and I would always be a fat guy.

You will notice that four of the sentences in that last paragraph begin with the words, "I told myself…" I was having these internal conversations with myself on a daily basis. I was feeding myself a line that misery, shame, and early death were my game plan for myself. Well, there I was, eating poorly, never exercising, and achieving my very own self-fulfilling prophecy. I had a nightmare for a goal, and I was hard at work making my "dream" come true. What causes our internal dialogue, our own personal "conversations with ourselves" to destroy our dreams of success and happiness and sideline us from our goals?

Even if you are wearing size 32 slacks right now or a size 4 dress do not think that this negative internal dialogue has no bearing on your own life. This process transcends losing weight and carries over into every part of your existence. How many times have you heard yourself make the following statements?

- There is no way I can save enough money to retire.
- My wife and I will never see eye to eye on anything again.
- My boss hates me and I will never get that sales promotion.
- Going back to school for my MBA will never happen now with three kids.
- We both work full time and we will never be able to save for a down payment on a home.
- I would love to get back into shape but I don't have time for a gym membership.

My personal fitness coach, David Greenwalt, calls this kind of negative self-talk "stinking thinking." We have to condition ourselves to be careful what we say to ourselves and what we say out loud to others. We actually hear ourselves think and say these things, and our brain really thinks that they are our future game plan. We begin to perform in ways to meet our low expectations. Our new motto becomes the cliché, "Avoid Disappointment: Aim Low."

In my first year of losing weight and changing my life, I began to recondition myself to think that certain things were possible for me again. I moved from a "victim" mentality to a "victor" mentality. I went from an external locus of control to an internal locus of control. I was believing for the first time in my life that I controlled the events in my life. I began to consider the possibility that I could even lose hundreds of pounds and weigh around 150. I was planning to be the greatest example of physique transformation ever. I was going to lose 250 pounds and I knew it was going to happen. Size 32 slacks. Rippling muscles. Speedo swim trunks at the pool. Running four miles three times a week. I was having those conversations with myself, and in every one of those talks I was succeeding.

Little did I know, but there was a monster under the bed. On October 1, 2001, one year to the day after I began this journey, that monster decided to crawl out from under the bed and try to kill me.

On that fateful day, I was at the Northeast YMCA engrossed in my workout. It was leg day. Extensions, curls, seated curls, dead lifts, and barbell squats. It was a real effort to finish this workout. I sat in the sauna for a while and still felt bad. I got in the pool to swim laps. I swam the first one and I felt bad. I kicked off the end of the pool with the ball of my right foot to start my second lap and my arms locked up. I got a stabbing pain right in my breastbone and I could not move my arms at all. I floated upright and asked the lifeguard for some help. I had hurt a rib doing those 215-pound barbell squats. I had torn a muscle and it hurt like hell. Yeah. That's it, I told myself. I tore a muscle. I went to the hospital to get checked out. The EKG ruled out a heart attack. The blood work ruled out a heart attack. They kept me overnight for observation. The third set of blood work told the tale. Dr. Doom came into my room to lower the boom. I had indeed suffered a myocardial infarction, a medical term for what every man over 40 fears the most, a heart attack. I was scheduled for a cardiac catheterization the next day. Dr. Doom returned with even worse news. I was going to require a quadruple bypass heart procedure. I had two hours to get ready.

I was devastated. The one thing that upset me the most was that I had allowed myself to get all excited again about losing weight. I had sworn to myself that I would never put myself in that position again. I had worked so incredibly hard for a whole year, but I got caught. My past sins had come back to haunt me. I had been warned by doctors my whole life that if I ever had to have heart surgery, I would not survive. I had to sign that legal consent form knowing full well in my heart, my damaged heart, that tomorrow would be my last day. I felt such rage that I really did not even care.

You will have that time in your life when your knees will buckle beneath you. The phone call in the middle of the night. The policeman at the front door at 2 a.m. The "I just don't love you anymore" letter. The pink slip in your mail slot at work. The lump under your right breast.

How will you get through the next ten minutes, the next ten days, the next ten months, the next ten years?

The conversation that you will have with yourself at that time will determine whether or not this incident will cripple you forever.

Well, I did not die. I survived and I am alive. Not just breathing with a pulse, going through the motions, waking up and going to bed, but *alive*! I came through with flying colors. My recovery was record-breaking. Breathing on my own the first night. Walking the hall the next morning. Working out with dumbbells at home ten days later. Swimming laps again in ten weeks. Bench pressing again in four months. I made it.

I found out why. I had wondered for a whole year. My reason to begin my transformation had dumbfounded me. The reason why I joined the YMCA had remained a mystery to me, It was as if God had put me in my car and that car had driven itself to the YMCA. The doctors told my family that if had not lost that first 90 pounds the cardiologists would not have been able to operate on me that day at 422 pounds. They would have given me medication and sent me home to die in two weeks. At 332 pounds, they felt confident enough to proceed. That was it! God had sent me on a mission one year ago to begin the process to save my own life. How cool is that? I got to save my own life.

I also got a once-in-a-lifetime opportunity to witness a miracle. There is no greater miracle in the world than the body's ability to heal itself after a trauma. Likewise, there is no greater trauma in the world to the human body than a group of people taking a chain saw to your torso and playing volleyball with your heart for five hours.

I have continued to lose weight. I will soon be closing in on having lost 200 pounds so far. This whole story is what propelled me into a speaking career and has finally gotten me published nationally after so many years of writing. This story is just too good to keep to myself. My message as I speak across the USA is simple but true. You are never too old, too fat, too weak, too sick, too many kids, too far gone, too out of shape, or too anything to change your life. You simply change the conversation that you continue to have with yourself about why you think that fate has a master plan to keep you down. That is the aforementioned external locus of control, the feeling that your destiny lies in someone else's hands. Let's look at some reasons for those negative conversations.

When I speak publicly, everyone asks me the reason why I let myself get so far gone. How does someone eventually get to over 400 pounds? Our bad habits do not just jump on our back in.the course of 24 hours. Liza Minnelli did not wind up at the Betty Ford Clinic the first time she consumed a pitcher of martinis. Gamblers do not lose their homes the first time they lose $50 at Hialeah. Robert Downey, Jr. did not go to prison for smoking one joint. Destructive habits, like abusing food and a sedentary lifestyle, sneak up on us one day at a time until they become ingrained into our psyche. We tell ourselves that they are not a problem. We tell ourselves that no one else is even noticing. We tell ourselves that we can get ourselves under control any time we want. We tell ourselves that our bad habits are not really adversely affecting our lives. Once again you will notice that the "we tell ourselves" conversations are the most negative and destructive psychological conditioning that we can inflict on ourselves.

I can honestly say that self-confidence, self-esteem, and self-image do not have any scale-weight milestones. I did not feel cocky and arrogant at 299 pounds and then humiliated and ashamed at 300 pounds. I continued to feel bad about myself even after losing 120 pounds. I could not perceive a change in my self-image. My physical body was becoming smaller than my brain could accept. This is the antithesis of anorexia nervosa. Sufferers of that disease look in the mirror and their self-image visual is actually stronger than their power of actual vision. Their actual vision tells them one thing, but their self-image still sees excess weight. I would look in the mirror after losing 100 pounds. Before I even got to the mirror I would already have my ingrained image of how I had looked for twenty years and was unable at first to acknowledge any real changes. I was not only telling myself that I had not really lost any weight, but my distorted sense of reality was backing me up.

Two years into my transformation, my life just began to explode in every aspect of my life. I came to grips with the fact that yes, I had lost a lot of weight. I could see it in my new driver's license, my new YMCA membership card photo, and my profile in my fitness coach David Greenwalt's book, *The Leanness Lifestyle*. I decided to push the envelope. Just how far could a guy wearing size 60 slacks go to prove what was possible? What goals were realistic and what goals were just too crazy? How many things could I achieve with my newfound fitness levels if I ruled out all the limiting and negative conversations with myself? Could a guy who once weighed 400 pounds actually wear bicycle shorts and Speedos?

Being profiled in David Greenwalt's book was a big deal for me. I was proud and honored for sure. It was a testament of my coming full circle. There I was on page 191, in front of God and everybody, in before and in-progress photos. Hundreds of thousands of people were going to see a photo of me at my worst without a shirt on. *My greatest fear in the world!* Two years ago if you saw me without my shirt on, it meant only one thing: I had to have you killed. Now it is just a conversation with myself. That was in the past, Mark. Your past no longer dictates your future, Mark. Your new lifestyle of eating healthy and working out daily will take you to your goal, Mark. I continue to feel better about my body and my self image as I continue to improve. I took thousands of pictures of me the first six months. I had to have another of those internal conversations. I had to let myself be embarrassed, humiliated, and ashamed at times to continue to improve. Treadmills stopped when I got on them. There were three different Cybex weight machines that I could not fit into when I started. I had to have help getting up out of the leg press machine. At 345 pounds, I stripped down to my underwear and was lowered into a dunk tank to undergo a hydrostatic body fat testing. These things were difficult and humiliating at times. At 270 pounds, I stripped down once again to have a Pro-Tan suntan application painted on my *entire* body at a local spa to have some professional progress pictures taken by a physique photographer. I knew that I had to endure these things if I wanted to get to my final goal. Too often we tell ourselves that we cannot achieve certain things because of the level of discomfort or distress involved. "I may be miserable but at least I am comfortable in my box," we say. But I had to have those awful fat and shirtless pictures developed and that body fat calculated in order to gauge my progress and to show others how far I have come.

There were all kinds of things that I wanted to try when I became much smaller. Some of these things were not psychological limitations, but the result of actual weight limit restrictions. For example, I began to ride roller coasters again. In August of 2001, I sat down in the Son of Beast roller coaster at Paramount's King's Island, the lap bar locked shut, and I was riding a wooden coaster again for the first time in over 15 years. I stayed at a Walt Disney World resort in May of 2002 and signed up to go parasailing. I lifted off a jet ski boat and soared to a height of 610 feet and flew for thirty minutes as I parasailed over Bay Lake at Walt Disney World. I wore a pair of Speedo swim trunks at the Polynesian Resort grotto pool at Walt Disney World that same summer. One month later I performed a tethered skydive out of an airplane in Frankfort, Kentucky. You have to weigh under 270 pounds to go up. (They actually weigh you to be legally safe.) I slide easily into restaurant booths. I buy pants in regular department stores. I told myself that all of these things were possible only if I stuck to an "impossible" change of lifestyle.

I really started taking even bigger risks in the areas of self-confidence and self-esteem. I jumped onstage one night almost two years ago and sang karaoke for the first time. That took courage like I have never known in my life. I started taking Body Pump aerobic classes and even signed up to perform onstage at the Louisville Fitness Expo. Did any of those people in that audience have any idea that the chubby guy up on stage bench pressing barbells to Guns ' n ' Roses "Sweet Child of Mine" had just five months ago undergone a quadruple bypass heart procedure? I appeared on local radio for one hour to talk about my story. I even got to meet and talk to Lou Ferrigno at the Arnold Fitness Classic in Columbus, Ohio and tell him what I was trying to achieve.

Communication remains a vital force in my life to keep me going toward my final goal. I have developed leverages to guarantee my success at whatever goal that I aim for in my career. Leverages are those situations that I put myself in to remove failure as an option. How many goals have you set wherein you were the only person aware of the goal? I had dieted many times in the past and never told a soul about my plans. In my heart, I knew that I would revert back to eating whatever I wanted in a few weeks, so I left the back door open for me to bail out without anyone's knowing. I was preplanning my failure.

The entire planet knows about my weight loss now. I have a ten page website at www.markgetsitdone.com with over 10, 000 hits so far. People from as far away as South Africa, Korea, and New Zealand e-mail me to check on my progress. I have been on radio and television, speaking to thousands of people so far about my story. I am writing a book entitled *The Weigh Out,* chronicling my ordeal. I am using the process of communication to have the whole world checking on me to safeguard my success. If I quit now, I would have to move to Jupiter. I even made a deal with my employees at work that if they catch me eating one bite of anything I should not have, such as candy, I owe each of them $20 every time they see me. Each speech, seminar, or keynote address I deliver is a catharsis to keep me energized. I feed off telling this story.

Leverages will work for you too as you commit to goals. I have a friend, Scott, who promised his three kids a new toy every Friday if Daddy had lost his targeted two pounds that week. They threatened to knock Daddy's head off if old Scott ate even as much as a cookie during the week. A book customer of mine, Ted, offered his coworkers $10 every time anyone caught him smoking a cigarette and his wife $100 if she caught him. Offer to cut your neighbor's yard for an entire summer if you do not have that deck project completed by April 1. You will be surprised what you can accomplish if you just state your goals out loud to other people and have them put your feet to the fire.

I set a "crazy" goal for myself in the summer of 2002. In an effort to challenge the accepted norm of possibility for a man in my former shape, I decided to become certified as an aerobics instructor. I used every bit of internal dialogue, positive self-talk, and leverage that I could dream of to tackle this goal. I had everyone at the YMCA, my support team at David Greenwalt's Leanness Lifestyle organization, my work colleagues, and my audiences cheering me on. My YMCA friends helped coach and train me for the requirements. David said that I *could do this*! My friends were skeptical beyond belief. The point is, I would have backed out of this early on if I had not relayed this goal to everyone. I knew I had to go through with it. I passed! I weighed 247 pounds that day and I did it. I remain to this day the only person ever certified by the Aerobics and Fitness Association of America as an aerobics instructor who has had a quadruple bypass. It remains to this day as my greatest achievement as far as stepping "out of my box."

I am about two-thirds the way to my goal. I have already achieved so many of the things that I sought to accomplish. I must now challenge myself to even higher and more outlandish goals. I must ask you now, what is "too crazy" for someone like me? I thought two years ago that twenty things that I have accomplished so far were labeled "too crazy." I want to get all the way down to 150 pounds. I want to appear on "Oprah" and impress the hell out of her. I want to testify before Congress about appropriating more money for obesity and diabetes research. I want to audition for Chippendales. I want to enter a bodybuilding show and compete in the 45-49 age men's category and win my classification. I want to be in the National Speakers Association Hall of Fame.

I will never again apply a label to myself because I have done that for far too long and it has kept me down. Karaoke? Mark, you know you cannot sing! Aerobic teacher? Mark, you know you have coronary artery disease! Skydive? Mark, you know you get a nosebleed on the top step of the ladder! Give a speech to 732 doctors? Mark, you know how low your self-esteem is! Talk one on one with Lou Ferrigno? Mark, you know how bad you feel about the way you look! Those internal conversations that seemed to disqualify me for everything in life are a thing of the past.

I encourage you to remove every label that you have applied to yourself that holds you down. That big, imaginary Post-It note™ that you wear on your forehead that says that you will never be able to lose weight, remarry, get back in shape, learn to swim, save for retirement, dance, sing, go back to school, understand your kids, quit grieving, forgive your spouse, start a business, write that book, or a million other things that you perceive as a lost cause.

I leave you with my favorite piece of advice, the one that ends every one of my speeches:

"Just one time in your life, just once, go do something that everyone says that you will never ever be able to do."

ABOUT MARK DRURY

*M*ark Christopher Drury is a man on a mission to reclaim his health by setting a goal to lose over 250 pounds. His speeches, seminars, and keynote presentations explode with his tales of self-discovery and reMARKable successes as he approaches that staggering goal.

He has been featured in David Greenwalt's book, The Leanness Lifestyle, *has co-authored three books of inspiration and humor, and is the author of his own personal triumph. Mark shares with his audiences his fears and failures of past attempts to conquer this demon. He also tells of going from 422 pounds to radio, television, aerobic instructor certification, parasailing, singing, professional speaking, authoring books, bodybuilding competition, and an ever-widening array of once-impossible goals. He can be reached at markdrury@markgetsitdone.com or at www.bluegrassspeakersbureau.com Learn more about him at his ten-page website at www.markgetsitdone.com anytime. Mark has a story to tell and he wants you to hear it.*

Contact Information
Mark Christopher Drury
9211 Hampton Ridge Court
Louisville, KY 40220-2982
Phone: 502-693-7598
Fax: 502-749-6608
E-mail: Markdrury@markgetsitdone.com
Website: www.markgetsitdone.com

IT'S NOT WHAT YOU SAY; IT'S HOW YOU SAY IT:
Using You and I Messages in Effective Communication

by Dovie Wesley Gray, Ph.D.

C ommunication can be defined as a message, verbal or nonverbal, sent and received between two or more persons with a clear understanding. The problem lies sometimes in the key word, "understanding." It is not what you say; it is how you say it. This chapter will illustrate effective methods for communicating using you and I messages to emphasize pertinent information. Utilizing these methods can improve the lines of communication within the workplace and improve public relations. Another benefit of using you and I messages is that your personal feelings are conveyed clearly.

Our first communication begins in the home setting before we enter the workplace. It begins with our parents and siblings, and continues with our friends, spouses, and children. At times, what we say is not what people hear. During my teenage years, when I was given a command by my parents to do a particular chore, I simply did it without question. At least, my parents never heard my comments. My comments were often spoken quietly and under my breath because it was understood that I was not allowed to talk back to my parents. Opinions were options for adults only. However, since I was the youngest of eleven children, I was allowed more liberties than my other siblings. My sisters and brothers often tell me that I got away with murder. I have always been inquisitive, and I began at an early age to communicate with my parents and with my other siblings, asking many questions.

That pattern carried over into my school years, and I soon became a leader in my school. During those formative years, growing into my own, I learned that communication was a powerful tool. I became an English major and often joined in debates and school plays. Along with learning the power of words, I studied human behavior and body language as they relate to communication. It was easy for me to read the expressions on my mother's face to know whether I was in a little trouble or big trouble. It became a game for me to read not only my mother's behavior and facial expressions, I also discovered that I could do the same thing with my siblings, friends, and my teachers. With an increased interest in discerning personality development, I was prompted to become a counseling psychologist, with special expertise in working with children and parents.

Behavior is learned. Therefore, if we have learned bad behavior, it can be unlearned. Likewise, if we have learned bad communication skills, we can learn how to communicate effectively, correctly, and well. What we learn as children and young adults carries over into our personal and professional lives. When I became a wife and a stepmother, communication took on a whole new meaning. My husband and I have a beautiful relationship, and I believe that we communicate well. There is only one topic that is taboo: my weight. He is a wonderful man who loves me unconditionally. However, when we discuss my weight problems, there is a true lack of communication. For example, when he says to me that I look super and everyone is not meant to be small, what I hear is, "Accept your big, fat self and move on." Or, he may say, "Maybe you just have big bones;" what I hear is, "I married an Amazon woman." Did he say that? Of course, he did not. Even with the best intentions, there is no way that he is going to be able to communicate his loving message to me because I have already heard and processed what I expected to hear. It does not matter how loving his tone is; he is not going to win that one. He truly means no harm. There are times that he just needs to nod and listen. That's one of those times! Because of my training, I am able to express my feelings to my husband clearly. However, I know that there are many husbands and wives who may experience communication difficulties. I would recommend professional counseling for those couples.

My stepsons gave multidimensional meaning to the word communication. They are wonderful young men now. As teenagers, they were from a different planet; they almost made me forget all of my professional training. I love them dearly, and they are now parents. (Justice is sweet.) I learned early in the marriage that the methods my parents had used on me were not going to work with my sons. Remember when I told you that I did what my parents told me and mumbled under my breath, a quiet whisper? Well, my youngest son reacted differently. I was fortunate that he was never rude or disrespectful, but completing a task when I wanted it done and when he wanted it done was like communicating in two different languages. If I asked him to do the dishes at six, he would do them at midnight or the next day. This was not a problem for him, and he could not understand why I turned red and raised my voice to a demonic tone. I had to remind myself that it is not what you say; it is how you say it. When he did not come in or call by curfew time, this behavior was not a problem for him. My heart was pounding until I heard him come through the door, but he was fine. When I communicated my concerns to him, he thought that I had a problem.

I had to use all my resources to help survive this period in my life. We laugh about it now, but it was not funny when it was happening. I did not like the idea that my son was pushing my buttons and controlling my emotions. I would get angry every time I looked at those dishes in the sink. On the other hand, he was listening to music and talking on the telephone. What is wrong with this picture? It was during that time that I began to study more about you and I messages. I had covered this topic in all my academic studies, but now was the time to apply the principles. Those principles worked, and it was the most liberating experience in my life. I was no longer a prisoner in the teenagers' world. I had total control of one thing, me. Therefore, my reactions to my son's behavior changed. Therefore, if you are a parent, hang in there; it does get better. Turn you responses into I responses. For example, instead of telling my son, "You still have not done those dishes yet," I would say, "I feel frustrated when I still see dishes in the sink. I do not like feeling this way." Expressing my dissatisfaction in that way took the pressure off my son and gave me total ownership of my feelings. It made him think about how he was making me feel instead of my always blaming him.

The you and I messages carried over into my professional life as well. As a customer service representative for Southern Bell, (currently BellSouth), my job was to take incoming calls for telephone repair services. I had a set script and a supervisor listening in to my calls periodically to assure that I was providing the best public relations in assisting a customer. It did not matter how rude the customer was or what the problem was, my role was clearly defined: keep a pleasant voice in responding to all calls. I still remember that script: "Telephone repair service; may I have the number that you are reporting, please? Could you verify your name and address, please? What problems are you experiencing today?" I usually would smile on the call as if the customer could see me. I remember vividly one day when a customer was having a problem with her phone lines, and she made an unusual request as to when and what "type" of repairman would report to her home. I still had to respond in a cheery voice that we would get her services on as soon as possible, not knowing if my supervisor was listening on that call or not. As long as the customer was satisfied, the company was happy. It's not what you say; it's how you say it.

In all of my customer service positions, whether it was at Trust Company Bank, City of Las Vegas Human Resources Department, educator/counselor, or working as a professional speaker/trainer, the needs have been the same. One of my most valuable lessons, I learned from one of my students. My morning routine included standing in the hallways, telling young people to get to class, take off hats, pick up paper, or watch their language. One morning a young man walked over to me and said, "Dr. Gray, we don't mind you telling us what to do, but can you do it with a smile?" From that point on, I still maintained my daily routine, but I would begin my ritual with "Sweetie, do you mind picking up that paper" or "Honey, you are going to be late!" It made all the difference in the world. The students felt better about my giving them a directive, and I still accomplished my goals. In a work environment, however, I would recommend appropriate words to use other than sweetie or honey.

In general, clients/customers want to be treated with respect, want to be heard, and they want good service. However, clients/customers come to us with their own problems and baggage. You are not a mind reader; nor can you predict every situation. You can have your act totally together, but a person having a bad day could ruin everything for you, if you allow it. Therefore, when you are confronted with a difficult situation or a lack of communication, the only person that you can control is yourself. You make the decision as to whether or not you will allow someone to ruin your day. I have discerned that effective communication can save you. Voice tone and the emphasis that we place on words can totally change the meaning of our message. It's not what you say; it's how you say it. Look at the following examples. Place emphasis on the words in italic and see how the meaning changes:

1. I *loved* your presentation!
2. I loved your *presentation*!
3. I loved *your* presentation!
4. *I* loved your presentation!

If you are a person who speaks loudly, you will find that people will respond to you loudly. If you are a soft-spoken person, people will quiet down so that they can hear you. If you have an irate customer/client, the louder that person becomes, the lower your voice tone should become. Usually when an upset person confronts you, he or she is most likely going through some other personal issues that have absolutely nothing to do with you. You just become the target because you are conveniently in the right place at the wrong time. A normal reaction is to yell back or get louder when someone is yelling at you. On the contrary, respond softly and slowly; swallow first before speaking. Silence also gives the irate person an opportunity to calm down. Give yourself time to assess the immediate needs of the irate person, and understand that you have no control over that person's behavior. However, you have total control of your words.

If you are an employee in management or a supervisory position, these practical tips will help to improve your work environment. Understandably, the work environment is a product of its employees' principles and core value systems. In addition, there will be many times when getting the job done is the most important thing, and you may not feel like stroking egos or hurt feelings. Productivity is the desired result. However, if there is a communication problem in the office, chances are the workers will be less productive. What are some practical ways to use you and I messages effectively in your workplace to improve the environment? Listed below are examples of how you can turn a you message into an I message:

You message: "Quit turning your quarterly reports in late! How many times do I have to tell you?"

I message: "When I receive your quarterly reports late, it causes me to miss my deadlines. I become frustrated when I have to keep telling you the same thing over and over."

You message: "You are late again! We have already begun the meeting."

I message: "I am really disappointed that you were late for the meeting. I could have used your input."

You message: "Turn down that radio! Can't you see that I am on the phone? You're so inconsiderate!"

I message: "I feel frustrated when the radio is so loud because I can't hear what the caller is saying."

You message: "Sir, will you please have a seat? Can't you see that I am working with another customer?"

I message: "Sir, I will be glad to assist you as soon as I finish with this customer. I understand that the line is long."

You message: "You always have something to say. When are you going to become a team player?"

I message: "I feel uncomfortable when there is opposition among our team. I know that I feel better when we are in accord."

You message: "You never recognize my work. You never have anything nice to say."

I message: "I am disappointed when I am never recognized for the things that I do for the company. I would like to hear something positive about my performance."

You message: "Can't you pull your salespeople together? You haven't met your quota in two months."

I message: "I understand that the economy is slow, but I am getting frustrated with all of the excuses."

The I messages give you total control of your own emotions; you are not blaming anyone else for your situation. Even though the initial problems may still exist, your reactions to them will be different. When you take the emphasis off the you person in the equation, it will force that person to reevaluate himself. The you person will already have a certain expectation of you, and you will deliver the element of surprise by not overreacting. Understand that this practice is a learned behavior, and it is not an easy one. A normal response is to become emotional, irritable, or impatient when tasks are not completed in a timely manner, but if you practice using you and I messages, communication will improve within your company or organization. Even if the you person has messed up, he will not feel as if you are attacking him because you are sharing your feelings. You have chosen to feel a certain way; the you person cannot make you feel anything. I can vividly remember when a parent came into my office to share that her daughter had a seizure disorder, and she said, "You would not understand." That parent was ready to defend her daughter's condition, and she truly believed that I could be a problem. Imagine the shock on her face when I replied, "Yes, I understand; I am a seizure patient, too." She no longer saw her daughter as a victim; she viewed her as a person who could be successful because she was looking at a person who was surviving with the same condition.

Believe me, I understand that this method is not a quick fix for all of your communication problems, but it will guarantee that your employees will feel better about themselves. Plus, they will view you in a different light. It takes practice, and it may feel weird at first. Try turning the following examples into I messages:

You message: "You are always complaining about working the third shift! Be thankful that you have a job!"

I message:

"_____."

You message: "You are not being fair; you gave me a bad evaluation."

I message:

"_____."

You message: "You need to work on your customer service skills; we are getting too many calls."

I message:

"_____."

As stated at the beginning, communication is conveying a message to a person or audience with understanding. How you say your words, coupled with your body language, determines if your message will be received. It's not what you say; it's how you say it. There is a difference between communicating and having a conversation. Effective communication includes a positive attitude, a willingness to listen to your customer/client, and a meaningful exchange of ideas. Focus on developing an interactive, collaborative working environment. Believe in the power of your words. Consistently communicate in a positive manner. The more you practice using I messages, the more comfortable you will become. Encourage your employees to be real with their feelings and model effectual communication for them. Affirm your feelings, and express them openly. Disclosing your feelings in an I message is not a sign of weakness; it can have a positive effect on your audience. Therefore, this method works whether you are in top management, midlevel management, supervisory positions, or an employee.

In addition, this method applies to your personal life as well. Try it with your spouse, children, or close associates. If you have been exposed to this concept before, begin utilizing it again. If this is your first experience, embrace the concept and enjoy the change. Examine your work and personal situations and think about how you could approach those situations differently. Incorporate I messages in your spoken and written communication. When you take ownership of your feelings, you gain control of your emotions. Remember, it's not what you say; it's how you say it. Maintain and respect the power of your words.

ABOUT DOVIE WESLEY GRAY, PH.D.

*D*r. *Dovie Wesley Gray believes that in order to understand other people's struggles and successes, it is important that she be transparent in sharing her own challenges. Some of these challenges include acceptance into graduate school, a move to Atlanta (by bus in 1974 with only $100 to her name and no place to live). Dr. Gray is an encourager, a motivator, and an inspirational leader. She has a passion to help people live stronger, fuller lives. Her optimistic attitude assists her in being an excellent teacher, a confident counselor, and a professional speaker. She teaches others how to find humor in even the most trying situations.*

Dr. Gray is the founder of Wesley Motivational Training Consultants, Inc., a practice that conducts seminars, workshops, and keynote speeches. Her passion for helping others is apparent in her personal stories and humor. Dr. Gray is a cheerleader for many, especially teachers, and she encourages educators to remain in the profession. She has been an educator and counselor for the DeKalb County School System (Georgia) for over twenty years.

Dr. Gray is the co-author of two books, Communicate Confidently, Clearly, and Credibly *and* Success is a Journey. *She holds a bachelors degree in English from the University of Arkansas at Pine Bluff, a masters from Clark Atlanta University in Guidance and Counseling, an Ed.S. degree from State University of West Georgia, and a doctorate in Counseling Psychology from the University of Sarasota.*

Contact Information:
Dovie Wesley Gray, Ph.D.
President & CEO
Wesley Motivational Training Consultants, Inc.
4115 Oxford View Court
Decatur, GA 30034
Phone: 404-284-5704
Cell Phone: 404-354-1755
Fax: 404-284-6524
E-mail: dovie@wesleymotivational.com
Website: www.wesleymotivational.com

PLATINUM PARTNERSHIPS:
Seven Strategic Secrets for Competitive Advantage and Lasting Business Results

---

by Terry Adams, M.Ed

*When businesses form partnerships,
they can serve clients in amazing ways.*

Would you like to increase revenue without adding staff? Want to attract clients that have seemed out of your league? Have you ever lost business because the client wanted a larger organization with more experts on staff?

If you answered yes to any of these questions, you want to start forming partnerships so you can get that business in the future. Informal or formal, short-term or long-term, partnerships are a great, low-cost way to overcome client concerns about size.

This chapter explains what partnerships are and how they can be the key to winning more business. But even more important is that it shows you how to build and maintain partnerships so your business can grow.

What Are Partnerships?

Partnerships are formal or informal business arrangements in which two or more individuals or companies combine their expertise to gain a more competitive advantage in getting new business or in satisfying a broader range of client needs than each could do independently. Partnerships can be formed by consultants, small businesses, and giants listed on the Fortune 500, in any combination that works for the partners and their clients. They can exist for the length of one assignment or project, or they can continue over the lives of the businesses involved.

In my consulting business, I specialize in helping clients in the financial services industry increase sales and retain customers. When my clients need expertise beyond what I offer, say designing marketing materials or purchasing promotional products, I combine my efforts with one or more partners to offer superior service to those clients. On a larger scale, companies like Xerox, Motorola, Boeing, Honda and Raytheon frequently combine forces with other giants to compete for public and private contracts that, by themselves, they would never be able to win.

What Are the Benefits of Partnering?

There are many benefits to be gained from joining forces with one or more partners. Large companies, such as the ones mentioned above, have been partnering for years. And that trend shows no sign of reversing itself. An article in the Journal of Business Strategy titled *"Creating Successful Alliances"* says, "A full two-thirds of companies surveyed by the Economist Intelligence Unit in 2003 expect their dependence on external relationships such as alliances, joint ventures, and strategic partnerships to significantly increase over the next three years. The reasons for this increase include the need for fast and low-cost expansion into new markets and greater control/influence of the customer relationship."[1] So, take it from the big guys: partnerships work!

Three of the best reasons to form partnerships are to get new business, retain clients, and be innovative. Let's look at each of these:

Get new business

The main reason to form partnerships is to gain new business that would otherwise be beyond your reach. That's a variation on the conventional wisdom that two heads are better than one, and that the whole is greater than the sum of its parts. For example, I was almost shut out of bidding on a sales training project because the client wanted to involve a variety of coaches. So I partnered with three other consultants I had worked with before and got the assignment. Similarly, if you are the lead partner (the one who is seeking other partners to fulfill a new client's needs), you can offer more services if you have potential partners at your fingertips.

Retain clients

Working with partners can also help you retain clients by offering them expanded service. Whereas previously they thought of you for "narrow" assignments involving only one skill or type of expertise, they will now begin to think of you and your partners as a full-service firm. This change in perspective gives you a competitive advantage in winning new assignments and a way to increase revenue without increasing your costs.

Innovate

Partners who are solo practitioners can spur each other to come up with innovative solutions to problems by contributing fresh ideas and different perspectives. This exchange occurs to me all the time in my business; I am always learning something from my partners about a project, industry, or market. One of my partners taught me that partnering with a sponsor to deliver a training program to a client with a limited budget can be a win for all: the client gets the training, the sponsor gets exposure to the client, and I get hired to do the project.

Are There Downsides to Partnerships?

With reward comes risk. That's true for most things in life, and partnerships are no different. Some of the pitfalls may only be annoying, while others have the potential to ruin your business.

Partnerships are more like a democracy (everyone has a say) than a kingdom (my way or the highway). In partnerships, you have to share decision-making responsibility and client fees. Because you are introducing your clients to your partners, there is always the risk of losing clients to partners. But the worst-case scenario occurs when your partners don't have the expertise they claimed, and they perform poorly for your clients. This result, in turn, damages your reputation and affects your future working relationship with those clients.

If you've ever worked on a team or committee, you know that when people work together, there's always the potential for disagreement and misunderstanding. The same is true in partnerships. A financial advisory partnership I was consulting with had set up roles and responsibilities to optimize the team members' expertise. One partner focused on investments and portfolio management; another focused on trusts, estates and retirement planning and the third focused on "rainmaking" (bringing in big clients). As the partnership grew in revenues, the rainmaker felt he was entitled to greater compensation because, if he hadn't brought in new clients, the partnership would never have made so much money. Because the three partners had only an informal agreement and had not clearly communicated expectations and other details, the partnership eventually dissolved, leaving each partner feeling betrayed. To diminish the potential for disaster, partners must learn all they can about each other and the expectations for the partnership early on. And they must be ever vigilant in the management of the partnership. The seven secrets below show you how to develop successful partnerships.

Seven Secrets for Cultivating Successful Partnerships

Effective partnerships take time and on-going effort, but the benefits are enormous. Trusted relationships need to be nurtured on a regular basis. Although there can be short-term monetary benefits, the real rewards come over time, just as they do with long-term clients.

If you are ready to learn how to develop these rewarding relationships, read on. The following seven secrets will show you how to develop, maintain, and grow platinum partnerships from silver and gold relationships.

1. Understand your partners.

No two people are alike. The more details you uncover about potential partners, the better equipped you will be to deepen the relationships.

Unlike working in a big company where you see the same people every day and get to know them through meetings and team activities, getting to know and understand partners is more difficult. But there is still plenty you can learn, even in casual conversations.

Ask questions

One good way to get to know potential partners is to ask open-ended questions. I use a standard set of questions, including:

What is your expertise and who are your clients or target audience?

Knowing the areas of expertise will help you develop complementary ways of working together. Knowing the audience will allow you to see possibilities of cross-selling each other's services.

How established is your business?

The answer will give you an idea of whether they are in business for the long haul and whether they will be there when you are ready to start working with them.

What do you hope to gain from the partnership, and what are your long-term goals?

Do they just want to make money, or are they interested in building long-term relationships to satisfy the needs of clients on an on-going basis? Coming from the same perspective helps you work more effectively together.

Whom have you partnered with before?

The response to this questions is how you "check references" to find out about ethics, values, reputation, and performance on other assignments.

Help your partners satisfy unmet needs

You can show your partners and their clients what they may have been overlooking all along. For example, I know a realtor who worked with her partner, a financial advisor, when he was having difficulty convincing clients of the benefits of downsizing to smaller homes as they approached retirement age. The realtor met with the clients to share her experiences and perspective, which reinforced the financial advisor's message. The partnership between the realtor and financial advisor ultimately served the clients' needs extremely well as they made retirement decisions.

2. Listen for partners' spoken and unspoken needs.

One of my favorite quotes about listening comes from Socrates: "Nature has given us two ears, two eyes, and but one tongue—to the end that we should hear and see more than we speak." Even in ancient times, it seems that people didn't know how to listen very well!

Listening is a rare skill, but one worth developing. By listening to your potential partners, you can begin to anticipate their needs. You will "hear" things that, although unspoken, are still communicated through body language, eye contact, posture, facial expressions or, in phone conversations, through pauses and changes in tone of voice.

Focus your attention on the conversation

Pay attention to both spoken and unspoken messages. Listen to what your partners are saying. If you are thinking about what you are going to say when they finish talking, they will sense it and interpret it as a lack of interest on your part. To stay engaged in the conversation, use the technique of paraphrasing, i.e., repeating the essence of what was just said using your own words. Summarizing periodically will also keep everyone focused and reinforce to your partners that you are paying attention and acknowledging the value of their contributions.

Make your partners feel special

Eliminate any distractions that might take your attention away from the people you are communicating with. If you plan to meet in person, arrange to have the meeting in a private, quiet place to avoid interruptions. Ask questions, based on what you already know about them, to show that you are interested in what your partners are saying.

Take notes

Taking notes aids in retaining information that potential partners share with you. When you remember an obscure detail, your partners will be impressed and realize that you care about them. You should always be looking for ways to meet your partners' needs and to add value, just as you would for a client.

3. Gain your partners' trust.

I've found that trust (between partners and between partners and clients) is one of the most important factors in an on-going business relationship. This conclusion is backed up by research reported in the California Management Review in an article called "Relational Quality: Managing Trust in Corporate Alliances."[2] The authors wrote about the importance of deepening trust over time to build strong partnerships because relationships are continually being tested and evaluated.

Since trust is so important, let's look at some ways to build and maintain it.

Show partners you are looking out for their interests

Be frank with your input, comments, and feedback. People will value your sincerity, directness, and honesty. For example, a partner and I were doing a needs assessment with a client and determined our skill sets weren't the best match. We were honest about our abilities and gave the business to someone else in order to ensure that the client's needs were met. We made a positive impression on that client, who has since entrusted us with many other consulting projects.

Follow through on all your promises

We all know how it feels when someone breaks a promise. The trust that may have taken weeks, months, or years to nurture can vanish in an instant. So say what you mean and do what you say. Think through what you are committing to, and if you don't think you will be able to deliver on your promises, don't make them. Get feedback during and after the project to keep the lines of communication open and to ensure that you and your partners are happy with the results.

When you make a mistake, admit it

Partners will forgive people who admit their errors. Take responsibility, remedy the situation, and figure out how to keep it from happening again.

4. Make it simple.

Business relationships can be complicated and frustrating. But if you've ever worked with a person who said, "Let me do that for you; it's no trouble," then you know the value of partnering with people who make your life or your project easier. Partners (and clients, too) will appreciate anything you do that simplifies their workload.

Speak their language

Don't "dummy down" information for your partners, but remember that not everyone is fluent in your industry's jargon. Who has time to learn another language just to get a project under way? Anticipate what partners will need to know, and present that information as simply as possible.

Simplify their lives

You become invaluable when you make people's lives easier by providing solutions to their problems, often by connecting them to other partners. One client's cash-poor, non-profit group wanted to advertise a fund raising event on local radio, and the radio station wanted to help but couldn't donate free airtime. The radio station approached a local car dealership whose owner agreed to sponsor the fund raising event by paying for the radio advertising time. The non-profit group got promotion for its event, the radio station got its fee, and the car dealership got exposure and subsequent good will by supporting a worthy community cause. All of the partners were winners.

Show them ways to innovate and streamline processes

As an outsider, you bring a different perspective to your partners' problems. You may see ways to save them time and money that they have overlooked simply because they are too close to the business. For example, I was working with financial advisors on ways to position themselves to reach affluent clients. When they revealed that their time was being consumed by administrative activities, I partnered with a professional organizer who established systems that would streamline their workflow.

5. Stay connected.

Partners (and clients) sometimes have short memories. Out of sight, out of mind. If you have not been keeping in touch, they may choose another partner simply because that partner was in touch more recently. So help them improve their short-term memories by keeping your company name in front of them.

Use technology to organize information about partners

Thanks to technology, there are easy ways to stay in touch. By using contact management software, such as ACT!, GoldMine, or Outlook, you can capture a lot of information about partners and clients. You can then use the calendar feature to remind you to call or e-mail them, or to send a post card or relevant article. Sending partners your online newsletter or monthly business tip is also a great way to stay in touch while giving them useful information.

In my business, I typically contact partners on a quarterly basis, sending them an article one quarter and an interesting web site address the next, then following up with a phone call the next quarter, and finally sending an educational piece the last quarter. I use my contact system to group them by profession (e.g., trainers, financial advisors, coaches) so I can use this same outreach system for a group of partners to save time.

Keep up with your partners throughout their life changes

In order to remain a resource over time, you will need to stay informed about your partners' life changes, no matter how much time passes between contacts. While talking to partners, update your notes in your contact system so you can identify ways to serve them in the future. Include information about their kids' college plans, their hobbies, favorite charities, job promotions, and new products and services they've developed, for example.

6. Educate your partners.

You can become invaluable to partners by being on the lookout for information that will make them more effective and efficient in their businesses.

Share useful information

People have access to a great deal of information, but often they don't have time to find what they need and read it. You can become a second set of eyes for them, looking for articles, conferences, and web sites that would benefit them. Or, if you've already solved a problem that they're struggling with, give them the solution. Don't make them reinvent the wheel. They can use the relevant information you've given them to make better decisions. In the process, you will be seen as a valuable resource.

How can you learn what's relevant to them? If you took notes while you were getting to know them (Secret # 2), and then entered the information in your database (Secret # 5), you already have an idea of what's relevant. You can also do research on your partners' industries to spot trends or changes they should be aware of. This not only gives you the opportunity to be seen as a resource, but to identify potential clients for you and your partners.

This concept of sharing ideas and information worked well for me when I gave a contract template to a partner who was able to quickly modify it for his needs. Using it saved him time and legal fees, and he was very grateful. He now sees me as a valuable resource, and this relationship has led to our partnering on several assignments.

7. Surpass expectations.

Before you can surpass expectations, you need to know what the expectations are. How do you do that? By asking questions and gathering information up front, before you even accept the partnership assignment, and then getting feedback on a regular basis during the assignment.

Clarify expectations

Throughout the life of the partnership, ask lots of questions. Never assume anything. In the beginning, ask potential partners whom they've worked with and what they liked about those relationships. Based on their previous partnering experiences, what would they like to do differently with you? What disappointed them? What were the most important lessons they learned from other partnerships? What worked really well? Hearing about their experiences with other partners and clients alerts you to what you need to do to make your partnership with them succeed.

Over-deliver

Do more than you said you would. It doesn't hurt to be a little bit of a perfectionist in meeting or surpassing partners' expectations. Send them a special thank-you gift for a collaboration that went especially well.

Surprise and delight

Delighting partners with excellent results reinforces trust, forges long-term bonds, and builds customer loyalty. Remember how good it felt the last time people you worked with went beyond the call of duty and delivered results beyond what you expected? It probably reinforced your positive impression of them and increased your sense of loyalty to them.

Customer loyalty, whether from clients or partners, drives profitability and growth. "A 5% increase in customer loyalty can produce profit increases from 25% to 85%," reports an article in Harvard Business Review.[3] The authors of the article also conclude that "the quality of market share, measured in terms of customer loyalty, deserves as much attention as quantity of share."

The greater the satisfaction, the greater the loyalty, which equates to client retention, repeat business, and more referrals. This is the essence of platinum partnerships.

Whether you are a solo practitioner or part of a small, medium or large business, you can use partnerships to increase your business. As you practice these seven secrets, you should be thinking about giving your partners reasons to praise you to others. Turn these relationships into walking advertisements for your business. If you follow this advice, your partners will have good things to say about you. And that's worth more than its weight in gold; it is worth platinum!

Notes:

1. Patricia Anslinger and Justin Jenk, "Creating Successful Alliances," *Journal of Business Strategy*, Vol. 25, Issue 2 (2004): 18-23.

2. Africa Areino, Jose de la Torre, and Peter Smith Ring, "Relational Quality: Managing Trust in Corporate Alliances," *California Management Review*, Vol. 44, Number 1 (Fall 2001): 109-127.

3. James L. Heskett, Thomas O. Jones, Gary W. Loveman, W. Earl Sasser, Jr., and Leonard A. Schlesinger, "Putting the Service-Profit Chain to Work," *Harvard Business Review* (March-April 1994): 164-174.

ABOUT TERRY ADAMS, M.ED.

*T*erry Adams has a reputation for driving sales and customer service through the roof for sustained business growth. She helps clients cultivate new business and increase customer retention while expanding referral sources. Terry models what she "speeches" by partnering with small to large size companies to ensure her clients achieve exceptional performance.

   Terry leads a management consulting practice that maximizes profitability and organizational effectiveness. Needs assessment is a major part of her initial contact with clients, evaluating internal and external influences to zero in on the key issues. She focuses on practical solutions using various methods including business analysis, process improvement, team development, coaching, and skills training to activate change. Her reputation as a dynamic and proactive strategic partner improves the bottom-line for her clients. Terry is a speaker, consultant, trainer and professional member of the National Speakers Association.

Contact Information:
Terry Adams, President
Adams Consulting Group, LLC
74 Wheatsheaf Lane
Princeton, NJ 08540
Phone: 609-430-9971
E-mail: terry@AdamsGroup.biz
Website: www.AdamsGroup.biz

COMMUNICATE
SO SOMEONE LISTENS

by Nan Siemer

Too many communicators believe good communication depends on the senders and/or their message. They take all the credit if communication is successful, and they are stressed out with guilt if communication breaks down. They pick the message, and regardless of the audience, they deliver it their way.

Yet, what if the message is never received? "If a tree falls in the forest and no one is there, does it make a sound?" If your audience isn't listening, are you really communicating? The answer is no.

The truth is, good communication is all about the receiver. The sender must give information someone wants in a way the audience wants to receive it.

Effective communication consists of a sender, a message, one or more receivers and constant, two-way feedback between the receiver(s) and sender.

Speaker

Audience

The Receiver

So, if it is all about the receiver, what does the sender need to do? First, the sender must do some homework, which involves conducting research on the receiver(s). Successful communication depends upon knowing your audience. Just because there is something you want to say doesn't mean anyone else wants to hear it.

I admire nuclear physicists, but I don't want to hear about the intricacies of their job. I have a nephew who is a nuclear engineering student. I love the kid, but I don't want to hear the details of his favorite class any more than he wants to hear about my latest home decorating project.

Too many senders think they know their audience, but the truth is they may actually know nothing about the receiver(s). Does the audience know anything about the topic or have a desire to know anything more? Do you have everyone's undivided attention, or are some of your listeners thinking about rush hour traffic or a sick family member? Is it the best time of day for someone to receive information?

Does the audience care? One of the biggest reasons for miscommunication is that the sender cares about the information far more than the receiver does. The key is to keep statements short and simple, be prepared to provide additional information if requested, and provide plenty of resource information if the receiver wants more. In other words, be flexible to make sure your audience is getting what it wants.

I work with scientific researchers who tell me it is impossible for them to share their years of research with the media in soundbites, which are only a few seconds long. My advice is to talk with the media as if they are discussing their research over a garden fence with a neighbor, assuming, of course, that the neighbor is not a scientist, too.

Another way to make sure you are giving receivers what they want is to ask. But be careful of getting that information from a third party! A middleman can cause rumors, misunderstanding, and miscommunication.

When I was a tour guide at the Arch in St. Louis, an inner-city class came to the Museum of Westward Expansion for a tour. As I discussed the westward movement in the United States, I sensed I was losing my audience. In desperation, I finally stopped the tour and asked the kids why they were not listening to me. One brave child boldly stated, "This museum isn't about me. There are no blacks in it." I explained I was not giving a "black history" tour, because it was not requested, but I began to point out pictures and quotes from blacks who were part of that westward movement, and for the rest of the tour the kids were pressing in close to me to hear what I had to say.

Know the members of your audience. And if you don't, get to know them before you have finished talking. Make sure the communication is successful!

Is the audience paying attention? Many times, attention deficit is not the sender's fault. It may be the receiver has something else to think about.

I regularly taught classes for the United States Information Agency, and I got to know some of the regular participants. One day, a regular came to class looking a little rumpled. Before the class started, he explained his wife had just come home from the hospital with their twins, and the babies had not allowed the new parents much time to sleep in the past week. He apologized in advance for how he might look or act. I told him if he dozed off, I would try to speak a little softer, but loud enough for the rest of the class to hear!

Think about September 11, 2001. How many of us really wanted to pay attention to anything except the latest news out of New York and Washington for the 24 hours (or more) after the terrorist attack?

I am a federal government trainer who was in Austria when the attack occurred. My students all worked for United States embassies in Canada, Europe, the Middle East, and Africa. For days, they were glued to their cell phones and computers. The best way to conduct our media training was to be flexible. We constantly refreshed the media headlines from the Internet and projected them on a screen in the classroom, and we added time for the participants to share with their classmates what was happening at their respective embassies.

If something gets in the way of your communication, don't ignore it. Embrace it!

Is it the best time to receive information? The time of day has a real impact on a person's ability to receive information. For example, the best time of day to have a meeting in the American business culture is usually at 10:00 a.m. and 2:00 p.m., never letting the meeting last more than an hour. Research has shown these are the times people are most alert during a regular workday.

The research shows that, by 11 a.m., people are starting to think about lunch and what they have to accomplish before their lunch break. Immediately after lunch, there is generally a tremendous energy dip, which lasts about an hour. Then, by 3:00 p.m., people start thinking about everything that needs to be done before they can leave for the day.

There are differences in other parts of the world. And even within our borders, there are people and places where the best time to communicate is the middle of the night.

I had a mentor for many years when I was a broadcast journalist. This man was a workaholic who got to work every morning around 1:00 a.m. and was usually in the office until after 5:00 p.m. But I learned that the best time to reach him was at 3:00 a.m. Although our conversations were always short, I had his undivided attention at that hour, and he always resolved my career crisis by sunrise on the same day. That's why any time I needed his help or advice, I would wake up at 2:30 a.m., drink some caffeine, clear my throat, and give him a call. Communicating with this man on his terms was the best thing I ever did for my career.

If your receiver is a morning person, and you are not, you might just have to adjust your sleep schedule on the days you want to communicate with this audience.

The Message

Create a message someone wants to receive. The audience wants to know, "What's in it for me?" And in an age of instantaneous, global communication, people usually want information immediately, and in as few words as possible.

One of the biggest mistakes made by communicators is they give too much information. They often know so much about a topic that they believe it is important to share every detail. Many audiences today simply want a summary that explains why the information is important to them and resources to find further information, if desired.

Face it, we are in a "fast food" society. We have information coming at us from all sides, 24 hours a day, seven days a week! We are often put in a position to want our information, like our food, fast.

I was speaking with a group overseas where the pace of life can be slower than where I live, outside Washington, DC. I was explaining that people are getting used to receiving information in shorter and shorter news stories on their radios and televisions. So, I explained, many are expecting the same of their daily conversations. One woman defiantly asked, "Just because they want information that way, does it mean we have to give it to them that way?" Surprised at her attitude, I shrugged and said, "Only if you want them to listen."

Again, the goal is to get people to absorb the information you want to communicate. If you are inflexible in your ability to deliver information the way they want to receive it, your message simply will not get through.

However, I am aware that it can take a lot of effort to compress a complicated issue into soundbites. Just as it takes patience to conduct years of research, it requires patience to whittle that research into a summary that can be absorbed by the general population. And if there are a few members who want more information, it's better to leave them with resources and your contact information than to lull the majority of your audience to sleep with too much information.

Simple . . . clear . . . concise; that's the type of language you want to use to get the best results from your communication. Don't waste someone's time sending unwanted information.

The Delivery

After you learn about your audience and what type of information everyone wants, you need to know how to deliver that message in the most effective way.

I worked for a man who would never return a phone call. Leave him ten messages, and not one would be returned by the end of the day. However, send him an e-mail, and you would usually get an immediate response.

There are advantages and disadvantages to every form of communication. Face-to-face is always best in delivering bad news or information that requires you to read the body language of the receiver, but it is not always possible to get together with your audience. Telephone conversations, while convenient, strip you of the ability to get non-verbal feedback and know if anything else is distracting the receiver from the conversation.

E-mails, while fast and able to be delivered 24/7 without disturbing the recipient, are impersonal and can be delivered before the sender removes errors and/or emotional outbursts, which can increase the risk of miscommunication. Text messages, because they are faster than e-mails, increase that risk. Faxes are a good way to get information quickly, but the quality of documents can suffer in the transmission. Regular mail, while slow, remains a wonderfully formal way to communicate.

It's also important to know that good visual aids can increase the absorption of your information. Research shows more than 75 percent of the population are visual learners, which means their retention of information is improved by good, visual images. So, if you do have a face-to-face meeting . . . or even an Internet conference call . . . you can enhance your message by using an effective Powerpoint presentation that includes good illustrations and not just screens of text.

The key is to find out what best suits your receiver. Good communicators today must be proficient with every form of communication. Their e-mails must be as polished as their telephone conversations or personal meetings. And they must know how their audience wants to receive information.

There are people who would give anything to be excused from a staff meeting. These face-to-face sessions with their colleagues can be excruciating. They compare standing before any audience to a slow and painful death.

Likewise, there are people who use their voicemail as a screening device. They hate to talk on the phone, which they use to gather information they can respond to in a way they prefer, such as e-mail.

The bottom line is that we are in an age when we receive volumes of information on a daily basis. We are constantly weeding through material to get to the information we need at any given moment. At times, this volume can be overwhelming.

I once trained a group of federal government employees, many of whom had duties which required them to monitor coverage in newspapers and magazines and on radio and television stations. I reminded them that in an Internet age, they must also monitor the Internet. One exasperated participant threw up her hands and said she simply had no more time in her day for any more monitoring!

You see, prophesies of death for newspapers and magazines in a radio and television era have not materialized. Likewise, we continue to have all of the before-mentioned information outlets, in addition to the Internet. As we create more ways of getting information, we also get more information! So, people are using their information delivery methods to pick and prioritize the information they want to keep.

Feedback

The only way to make sure you've been heard is to get feedback, and eye contact is the best way to get feedback. Even if the eyes are not the window to the soul, they are a good way to determine if someone is paying attention to you. Of course, this feedback can occur only if the sender and receiver are in the same room or on camera through video conferencing.

I watched a client give a presentation. He started speaking, and then went off into a "zone." He stared into space for his entire speech. He flipped through slide after slide of boring copy he had memorized verbatim. And when it was all over, he looked back at me like I had just walked into the room. I asked him what he was thinking about during his presentation, and he admitted he didn't remember one thing after starting his speech. He went into automatic pilot. His method of dealing with his discomfort in giving a presentation was to remove himself . . . mentally, if not physically . . . from the room.

Feedback throughout your presentation is critical. You need to know from the expression on the faces in the crowd if your message is getting through. And you need to encourage questions to make sure you and your audience are on the same page.

Some senders wait too long to adjust their message if they see they are losing their audience.

A client once said he knows he bores his audiences. When asked how he knows, he said he gets the message when "tears roll down their cheeks." I told him I suspect there was some earlier signs he had missed!

It doesn't matter the size of your audience. Granted, you're more focused on each other if there are only two people conversing. However, a communicator's job is to get a message to an audience, whether there is one or 1,000 people in the room.

Small audiences are usually more open with feedback. They feel the pressure to be more participatory with the communications process. Receivers are less likely to ignore a speaker or feel ignored in a small group. Therefore, feedback flows more freely.

It is harder, if not impossible, to reach every person in large groups. Therefore, a sender's goal shifts from engaging each person to reaching at least a vast majority. With large audiences, if most receivers get the key message(s) and retain the information for 48 hours, the communication process is a success.

If you are in front of a large audience and one or two people drift off to sleep, it could be they are sleep deprived or have some other problem that is out of your control. But if a number of people in the audience begin to nod off, the communicator needs to take action to correct the problem. There are hundreds of ways to engage your audience, from moving around the room to taking questions. The key is to accept the feedback of your receivers and respond accordingly.

Good communicators know how to create a good message. Yet, every GREAT communicator knows the essence of the craft is to focus on the audience. A communicator must know his audience and give the message in a way it will be not only received, but embraced. Getting and giving feedback ensures both the sender and the receiver are getting the same message.

It's all about the receiver. If a sender ignores receiver(s), there is a very good chance the receiver(s) will ignore the message.

ABOUT NAN SIEMER

*N*an Siemer is a born communicator whose skills complement her natural talents. She worked for 15 years as a broadcast journalist before striking out on her own in 1995 as a communication/media consultant. Her diverse communications background includes work in radio and television news, magazine, news wire and newspaper writing, as well as teaching various communications courses at the college level and training government and private sector workers.

In addition to speaking and training throughout the United States, Nan's work has taken her to South America, Africa, Europe and Asia. Her public speaking career began as a tour guide at the Arch in St. Louis; a job which helped fund her education at Lindenwood College in St. Charles, Missouri. She has an MA in Mass Communications and a BA in Broadcast Journalism. Today, she conducts training programs, gives speeches, and meets individually with clients on a wide variety of oral and written communications topics.

Nan is the founding president of the Radio Television News Directors' Association (RTNDA) Washington Area Chapter, a past president of the National Association of Women Business Owners (NAWBO) Capital Area Chapter and an active member in the National Speakers Association (NSA).

Contact Information:
Nan Siemer
BREAKERS
5906 St. Giles Way
Alexandria, VA 22315
Phone: 703-313-0147
Fax: 703-313-0172
E-Mail: breakers@erols.com
Website: www.BreakersConsulting.com

THREE KEY INGREDIENTS
TO EFFECTIVE COMMUNICATION

by Kim Robinson

A young woman is promoted to office manager, and her first order of business is to move the entire company into a newer and bigger facility. It is a huge task but she applies herself and takes care of everything on schedule. The day before the actual event, she orders a beautiful wreath of flowers with a welcoming ribbon across the middle, to be placed above the entrance for employees to see as they arrive for work in the morning. The next morning when she gets to work, the beautiful wreath is above the door. But the ribbon across the middle says, "Rest in Peace." The young office manager is mortified. She immediately calls the flower shop, gets the salesman on the phone, and expresses her outrage. After listening to her rant for a few minutes, the salesman finally blurts out, "Let's look at it from the other side. Somewhere today there is a funeral with a wreath above the casket that says, "Good luck in your new location."

This story illustrates the need for good communication in the sales process because no one wants to publicly wish the dearly departed good luck in their new location. Neither the young office manager nor the relatives of the deceased would ever want to do business with that flower shop again, all because the communication process at the flower shop broke down.

This chapter describes three key ingredients to successful communication in the sales process. These ingredients are: *enthusiasm, common sense, and attitude.*

Many people believe that to be a good salesperson it is necessary to be pushy or obnoxious, or that sales communication is simply a nice way of saying don't take no for an answer. What a load of rubbish! The overwhelming majority of people who make a great deal of money selling something are not that way at all.

Sales is a process of communication that anyone can master—that's right, *master*—simply by embracing a couple of beliefs. Whether the person is male or female, naturally gregarious or painfully shy, all it takes for someone to become a master salesperson is to first embrace the notion voiced by Zig Ziglar that you will get everything you want out of life if you just help other people get what they want. And, second, to *believe* the product or service is a *good value* and that it will enhance people's lives in some way, big or small. For example, a potholder for cooking may not appear to be much of a life enhancement. However, if it is of good quality and sells for a good price, and you come across someone who wants to avoid hand burns while cooking, then it is a good value and a product that will enhance someone's life.

This second belief, that what you sell is a good value, is more commonly known as my first point—enthusiasm.

Enthusiasm

An enthusiastic belief in your product does not mean that you should become a rambunctious cheerleader. Enthusiasm does not have to be loud or annoying to be effective. It only has to be sincere. A sincere *belief* in your product can be, and most often is, calm and professional, and it is the basis of enthusiasm. The reason belief is such a strong communication tool in the sales process and one of the top three ingredients to success in sales and to communication in general, is that it is contagious: if you believe in your product, others will too. And if others believe in it, they will buy it.

My wife and I needed, well, we *wanted*, new major appliances when we moved into our new home, so we went to a large appliance store to shop. All we needed when we arrived was a salesperson to help us get what we wanted, to show us our options, and to guide us through the buying process.

We entered the large showroom with its intimidating volume of choices, and all the salespeople glanced our way, ignored us, and left us to wander around.

After a while one of the salesmen finally approached, split his face with a 200 watt smile, grabbed and pumped my right hand with his, declared "Welcome to our fine store," and asked in a declarative manner, "Can I help you? " Startled, we managed to tell him we were considering the machine in front of us and, without wasting another moment, loosening his grip on my hand, or lowering the wattage of his smile, he steered us toward a totally different brand of machine. It was obvious to us that his enthusiasm did not extend to helping us buy what we wanted, but rather to get us to buy what *he wanted to sell*. His belief in his product extended only to the belief in the fat wallet he would have from the commission he would earn by selling us a high-end machine. His misplaced enthusiasm left him without a commission check at all because we took our business to another store.

At the next store we were warmly greeted by a salesman who got off on the right foot by asking us the perfect open question to begin the retail sales process, "How may I help you?" Not "*can* I help you" like the first guy. "Can I help you?" is a common starting point for both retail and inbound telesales people, but it is the wrong way to begin a sales conversation. It is wrong because it is a closed question that invites a yes or no response. If "yes," then another question must be asked to get the customer to speak; if "no," the conversation, and the sales process, is over.

"How may I help you?" on the other hand, is the right way to begin a sales conversation because it is an open question that invites conversation. Moreover, conversation is the most comfortable way to uncover customer needs. It is so important in the process of uncovering customer needs it is written on the back of the vests of every single employee of the world's largest retailer, Wal-Mart. This second salesperson was a professional who opened the conversation well by asking us to speak first and tell him our areas of interest. As he showed us our appliance options, it was clear that he believed his products were a good value and that we would benefit from the purchase of the high-end of the scale. His enthusiasm was contagious and we caught it. As a direct result of his calm, professional, enthusiastic belief in the high-end products his store offered, my wife and I spent a lot more money than we had planned to!

Best of all, he was right. We were, and still are, delighted that we spent the extra money to get the higher-end products. That salesman properly used enthusiasm to guide us into making a buying decision.

I once lead a direct sales team for a cable company in San Francisco. The sales representatives sold cable TV subscriptions door-to-door on a 100 percent commission basis. They earned a small amount for every new subscriber they signed up, but the dollar amount doubled if at least 40 percent of their new subscribers started with a premium movie channel like HBO or Showtime. Starting service for the new subscribers with a premium movie channel was a good value because it saved money on installation while providing a couple of hundred movies for just a few dollars. Because of its high value to new subscribers, it was a pretty easy sale.

When I took over the team, I inherited one salesman who was consistently in the top three for new subscriber sales but always last when it came to selling premium movie channels. His name was Larry and I quickly found out that he never achieved the 40 percent pay threshold. Never. Despite his sales volume he was barely making a living. I pulled him aside after I saw his performance history and asked him why he was not selling any movie channels. His simple answer was, "Nobody wants them in my territory."

I suspected the issue involved his presentation more than a conspiracy against the cable company, so I went out with him one night to see first-hand what he was saying in his presentations. Early on, a young couple invited us in to discuss getting cable. They took us into their kitchen, and we all sat around the table. I sat to Larry's left, the man straight across from him, and the woman on his right.

Larry explained my presence by introducing me as his assistant and he launched into his presentation. After just a couple minutes the man said, "Okay. Sign us up." Larry pulled out an order sheet and before his pen touched the paper the man asked, "What about HBO?" Larry looked at him and answered without hesitation, "You don't want HBO. It's no good. Save your money." I did not need to be a rocket scientist to figure out why Larry was not selling any movie channels! I could not wait until we were outside to provide him with the coaching his presentation so desperately needed, so I reached deep into the bag of old-school sales management techniques and pulled out...physical abuse. I kicked him. Hard. "Ouch!" Larry cried as I maintained an impassive poker face. The man and his wife looked askance at us both and did not really believe what had just happened, so the woman added, "Really? We heard HBO and SHOWTIME are pretty cool." Larry shook his head as he opened his mouth. I knew he was going to repeat his earlier warning, so, before he told them again not to buy what he was selling, I kicked him a second time. Harder. "Ouch! Stop that!" he cried.

Moments later we were out on the sidewalk, and Larry confessed as he limped along beside me that he simply did not believe HBO and Showtime were a good value, so he had a hard time selling them. I liked Larry, and I did not want to see him walk with a permanent limp, so I helped him find another job selling something else.

Both the appliance salesman and Larry are clear examples of the important role enthusiasm plays in communication and the sales process. Help people buy what they want, and believe in what you are selling. It is that simple.

Common Sense

The second key ingredient to successful sales communication is not to insult those with whom you want to do business.' Everyone naturally thinks it absurd to insult people as part of the sales process, but well-meaning salespeople do it all the time. I recently shopped for a new cell phone service, and, in almost every store I entered, the salesperson would approach and ask me the name of my current service; after I answered, they denigrated that carrier. In one store the sales rep actually pointed his finger at me and declared, "Big mistake!"

I like to think none of these salespeople believed they were insulting me. They most likely were victims of the common misconception among poorly trained salespeople that denigrating the competition elevates the quality of their own product. Actually, though, insulting something I have purchased is the same as insulting me directly.

No one wanted to know why I had purchased the cell service I had. If they had asked me, they would have discovered it was a good decision at the time, one deserving a compliment and not a reprimand. But even if it had been a dumb move, I certainly would not want anyone to point that out. The same holds true for those times when customers or prospects volunteer they made a mistake with an earlier purchase. When this happens, the natural tendency among rookie salespeople is to misinterpret that old, and incorrect, adage, "The customer is always right," and agree with them to establish a rapport. Common sense needs to come into play here because to agree with someone's self-deprecating remark is the same as to offer it up yourself.

A common sense rule in sales communication is to never insult someone's previous purchase or agree with his or her self-deprecating remarks about a previous transaction. Avoiding the former is easy, and a good salesperson can easily turn the latter into a positive communication tool and a true rapport builder simply by treating the customer's remark as *fishing for a compliment.* No one would think of agreeing with a spouse who comes home from the salon or barber and announce his or her haircut is awful. No, self-preservation kicks in, and we say something like, "Not at all, Honey. You look great." Do the same with a prospect by finding something to compliment about a previous buying decision. The compliment needs to be sincere and something like "Not at all. You made a good move then. Now it is time to modernize/update/re-examine/upgrade.

Attitude

The third key ingredient to successful sales communication is attitude. Our personal attitude is the lens through which we view the world and, as such, has a great deal to do with how we interpret and respond to life's challenges. A positive attitude leads to optimism, and an optimist tends to expect the best. We (I count myself an optimist) expect things to work out in our favor, and when they do not, because bad things happen to everybody, we deal with the situation as bad luck and move on, fully expecting things to get better because our luck is generally good. A negative attitude, on the other hand, leads to pessimism, and a pessimist tends to expect things to fail, to not work out. And when bad things happen, because bad things happen to everybody, they are viewed as self-fulfilling prophecies because they were expected all along. Pessimists often say things like, "Just my luck" when something does not go their way.

Part of my recruiting strategy with the team of door-to-door sales people I once led was to point to a half-full glass of water on my desk and ask each new hire how much water was in the glass. Immediate rejection with door-to-door sales is more common than with most sales jobs, and I preferred to hire people with positive attitudes. It was my low-tech glass-of-water attitude-measuring assessment test that provided me with a snapshot of how each person viewed the world. Were things on the way up, or were they on their way to the bottom. My test was simple and clichéd but accurate all the same.

The number one complaint among the sales reps who were not doing well on that sales team was territory. All the low performers claimed no one in their territory wanted to sign up for cable TV. Their further claim was that those sales reps who were doing well were doing so only because they had a better territory.

The entire sales team looked upon one territory in particular as terrible. No one had made a go of it, so it was universally viewed as financial death for a cable sales rep.

When I looked at the area, I could not understand why no one had been successful. It was a good working-class suburb with people who all had jobs, money and televisions, so it should have been a great territory.

I had just hired a young man who quickly identified the glass of water as half full, so I thought I would try something new. His name was Harris, and I pulled him into my office before he met the rest of the team and told him he was going to start in a terrific territory. I told him that, due to a recent staff shake-up (true—the previous sales rep for that territory had just quit from lack of sales), the territory I was sending him into was plum and that he could not fail to sign up new subscribers. I added that I could not promise him the territory on a permanent basis because he was new, and I did not want to anger the more veteran sales reps, but I assured him that he would have at least two weeks to do as well as he could before I might have to pull the plug.

The weekly quota was 15 sales and Harris wrote 5 sales that night.

He wrote 20 sales the first week and 25 the next, and every one of his new subscribers took at least one movie channel. Harris was making money. When I asked him at the next sales meeting the secret of his success he stated, "What do you mean? Everyone in the territory wants cable." From that moment on, the low-performers complained that Harris succeeded only because he had a great territory.

Harris was not the world's greatest salesman. Not by a long shot. He was young and right out of college, and he barely knew what cable television was all about. He succeeded where others failed because he expected things to work out. Rejections were simply bad luck to be shrugged off and the next door would be a sale. He expected things to go well and they did. His positive attitude powered him past the bad moments and enabled him to succeed. He embraced success and was successful. Those who had failed in that territory did not expect to succeed, so they interpreted rejection as a self-fulfilling prophecy, and they could not effectively move on. They embraced failure so they failed.

What a difference attitude makes.

If you accept the fact that no one can force you to be either positive or negative, then you must accept responsibility for deciding on the type of lens through which you will view and interpret the world and its challenges. This decision is made every day. And every single day before you leave the house I urge you to decide to be positive. Look yourself in the mirror as you dress and say, out loud, "Positive things happen to positive people, and I decide to be positive today."

In this narrative I used the sales process as the vehicle for illustrating the importance of enthusiasm, common sense, and attitude to effective communication. However, these three qualities should never be limited to guiding someone into make a buying decision. They are key ingredients to living a good and fulfilling life as well. I urge you to be enthusiastic about life, to exercise common sense in everything you do, and to choose to be positive every single day.

ABOUT KIM ROBINSON

Kim Robinson has been in sales all his life. He rose from a door-to-door salesman to a Senior Vice President of Sales and Marketing on the strength of good communication skills, common sense and a lot of hustle.

He left his last executive position in 2001 to launch SMMarT Solutions, a sales consulting and training company He claims that anyone with a pulse can become a master salesperson by learning his comfortable and permission-based sales process. SMMarT stands for Sales—Motivation—Marketing—Training and the company already enjoys a client base that spans the continent. He speaks professionally about communication and the consultative sales process, and his lifetime of success in sales combine with his dynamic presentation style to create highly entertaining and effective keynotes, sales training programs, workshops and seminars.

Contact Information:
Kim Robinson
SMMarT Solutions
14052 Lakeshore Drive, Suite 100
Des Moines, IA 50325.
Phone: 1-877-840-7425
E-mail: Kim@SMMarTSolutions.com.
Website: www.SMMarTSolutions.com

COMMUNICATE CONCISELY AND CREATIVELY, TOO!

by Len Lipton, Ph.D.

It's a no-brainer. You're more likely to be successful in life if you communicate clearly, confidently, and credibly. However, communicating clearly, confidently, and credibly may not be enough to insure your success. Why? Because in today's fast-paced, impatient, and constantly changing world, you must also communicate concisely. And, to stand out from the rest of the crowd, it helps if you can also communicate creatively.

Communicating Concisely

Whether you're communicating to boards of directors, executives, customers, clients, or colleagues, these important listeners don't have time to hear you ramble on and on. You have to get to the point and the bottomline as quickly as possible. "Time is money."

Whether you're communicating by e-mail, fax, telephone, or in person, your written and spoken messages must be as concise as possible yet complete and understandable.

Whenever you are communicating to groups large or small, first ask yourself, "What messages do I want to communicate to the audience?"

Assuming you had an hour or more to give your presentation, what messages would be good for the audience to know? Make a list of these *good-to-know* messages—approximately eight to ten points—on a separate piece of paper.

Now, ask yourself, "What messages must the audience know?"

If you had only ten or five minutes in which to give your presentation, what messages must the audience know?

From the first piece of paper with the eight to ten *good-to-know* messages on it, take one, two, or three of the essential, most important messages and rewrite them on a separate piece of paper with the heading, *Must-Know* Messages.

When you are limited to a short presentation, concentrate on communicating only one, two, or three messages to the audience. This way, the audience comes away with a clear, distinct message instead of being confused by information overload.

If you were to use this *good-to-know* vs. *must-know* technique for all of the presentations you will ever give during the rest of your life, the quality of your presentations would increase dramatically. Why? Because now you are focused and clear about what you must communicate in a very short time to a particular audience. You have prioritized your messages by their importance.

No matter how long or how short your scheduled presentation is, you must be able to communicate the essence, theme, or main message of your presentation in as brief a time as five minutes. That may be all the time you have to communicate your message.

Consider the following scenario: You've been asked to give a one-hour presentation as part of a day-long program for business executives. Several speakers are presenting that day. The speaker ahead of you exceeds his or her allotted time. The meeting planner asks you to cut your presentation by half in order to get the program back on schedule.

If you have memorized your one-hour speech precisely from beginning to end, having to cut your presentation could be a nightmare, resulting in your experiencing rapid heartbeats, sweaty palms, and difficulty breathing—a condition you obviously want to avoid.

In a situation like this, if you want to be perceived as a polished presenter, you need to be flexible. You need to be ready to deliver a shorter version of your hour-long presentation right on the spot.

Experienced presenters learn to communicate their messages in both long and short versions to meet the needs of the moment. Think of your presentation not as one long talk, but as a series of short, separate segments within a larger whole.

Think of your hour-long presentation as if it were the grand ballroom

Grand Ballroom   *Figure 1*

60
Minutes

Grand Ballroom   *Figure 2*

Salon F 5 minutes	Salon G 5 minutes	Salon A 10 minutes
Salon E 10 minutes		Salon B 10 minutes
Salon D 10 minutes		Salon C 10 minutes

in a modern hotel. With all the movable, inner-wall panels folded and hidden behind the permanent outer walls, the wide-open space within the grand ballroom represents your 60-minute presentation [see figure 1]. If you have an hour in which to speak, you have plenty of room (time).

By extending one of the movable wall-panels across the room, you've cut the one large space of your hour-long presentation in half. By closing off salons A, B, and C [see figure 2], you have about 30 minutes of space remaining, represented by salons D (10 minutes), E (10 minutes), F (five minutes), and G (five minutes). If you were to further close off salons D, E, and F, the space remaining (salon G) in terms of time would be about five minutes.

If you want to be perceived as a polished presenter, you need to create a salon G (or five-minute) presentation that contains the essence, theme, or main message you want to communicate.

With practice, you'll find it relatively easy to expand your salon G speech by opening up the moveable walls to include more salons (spaces or time) to fit the situation. If time permits, you can fill the space with personal stories, anecdotes, metaphors, exercises, demonstrations, role plays, and group activities.

Communicating Creatively and Clearly

In addition to communicating concisely, a polished presenter also communicates creatively.

The acronym SHAMPOO can help you in the brainstorming phase of designing your presentation. Each letter in SHAMPOO stands for a tool you can use to add a little luster and life to your presentations, making them more appealing to your audiences.

S = Stories	(Communicating Creatively)
H = Handouts	(Communicating Creatively)
A = Acronyms	(Communicating Creatively)
M = Metaphors	(Communicating Creatively)
P = Props	(Communicating Creatively)
O = Organization	(Communicating Clearly)
O = Overview	(Communicating Clearly)

Including Personal Stories

Personal stories help distinguish you from other presenters. Audiences will remember the stories and then your points if you use colorful, descriptive, specific language.

Months, even years after hearing one of your presentations, someone may say, "I remember you. You're the presenter who told the story about the 380-foot bungee jump, eating cherry ice cream, and finding the courage to take risks in life. That was a memorable story you told."

Organize each personal story in a concise manner. First, provide a time frame and describe the situation, the problem, or the challenge you faced: "Two years ago, I was ..."

Second, indicate the tasks you had to perform in order to deal with, handle, or overcome the problem or challenge. What were your priorities? Did you have to delegate some responsibilities to get the job done or complete the project?

Third, describe the action(s) you actually took. Did something unexpected happen that affected your approach to the problem? Was your budget cut? Did you lose a team member you were counting on? What did you do to overcome the unforeseen hurdle or obstacle?

Fourth, what was the result? How did the story turn out? What happened in the end? What was the lesson learned? What is the point of your story?

These four steps (Situation, Task, Action, and Result) can be reduced to an acronym: STAR (Situation, Task, Action, Result).

The next time you include a personal story in your presentation, use the STAR approach to make your story organized, concise, complete, and memorable.

And, if your personal story contains some humor, it's like icing on the cake.

Handling Your Handouts

Your handouts are leave-behind pieces for audience members to use during your presentation and refer to after your presentation. Ideally, handouts contain the important points in your presentation, a list of resources, and specific contact information. After they leave your presentation, audience members will be able to communicate with you and refer others to you.

Instead of your handouts consisting only of wall-to-wall words (all text with narrow margins), try adding graphics, charts, and diagrams. Visuals will punch up your words and add excitement.

Experiment by leaving blank spaces next to visuals so audience members can jot down their ideas. This way, your handouts become more interactive.

If your handouts contain a word-for-word rendition of what you are going to say, what is the incentive for audience members to stay and listen to you? People could just take the handouts and leave before you begin your presentation.

Because your fill-in-the-blanks handout materials require active participation from audience members, these attendees have a stake in what's happening. Without the added fill-in-the-blank information provided by the presenter during his or her talk, the handout materials are less meaningful.

In your handouts, include a resources section. Include relevant book titles and authors, as well as names, street and e-mail addresses, web sites, and telephone numbers of associations and organizations audience members can contact for additional information and materials. Adding this type of resource information increases the shelf-life of your handouts. It is more likely audience members will hang onto your handouts long after the day you delivered your presentation.

Using Acronyms

Acronyms are special words in which each letter stands for another word. Acronyms can help audiences remember the main points you are presenting.

What easy-to-remember word can you think of that contains letters that could stand for key words you want people to remember?

You're involved in an acronym now: SHAMPOO.

The A in SHAMPOO stands for acronyms. If your audience members can recall the acronym word, chances are greater they'll remember what each letter in that word represents.

Write down the *must-know* messages you want to communicate. Find the key word in each message. What letter does that word begin with? Can you form a word with the first letters of your key words?

By arranging the key words Stories, Handouts, Acronyms, Metaphors, Props, Organization, and Overview in this particular order, the first letter of each word forms the acronym SHAMPOO.

Using Metaphors

To what item, process, or concept can you compare the main point or idea of your presentation? It's easier for audience members to remember your point if you can help them visualize a clear image related to the point you are making: a metaphor, in other words. For example, if you want to emphasize that polished presenters need to be flexible, you could recommend they prepare several versions of a presentation to fit different time limitations.

Earlier in this chapter, I compared a planned hour-long speech to the space within the grand ballroom of a modern hotel, with all the movable, inner-walls or partitions hidden away. The total space within the grand ballroom represented approximately 60 minutes. By utilizing the movable wall panels, we could partition the grand ballroom into smaller spaces. As a result, we divided our hour-long presentation into separate segments, like smaller rooms within the grand ballroom. The grand ballroom and the smaller rooms within it are a metaphor for a presentation that is anywhere from five to ten to 20 to 30 to 60 minutes long.

Using Props

Props can be as varied as a newspaper article, photograph, magazine ad, hat, street sign, or travel poster. Props can be relatively small and easy to carry.

A prop can anchor a point you are making. A prop acts as a visual aid to make a point, story, or anecdote more concrete, more real. A prop is something the audience can actually see. It allows for a clearer understanding of a concept. For example, by using a special hat that is reversible, you can anchor (reinforce) the concept of flexibility. Showing the hat one way and then turning the hat inside out demonstrates another side, aspect, or look. It's not just one hat; it's two hats in one. It's flexible.

Whatever prop you choose, make sure it is relevant to your remarks.

Organizing Your Presentation

Does your presentation have a beginning, a middle, and an end? No matter how long or short your presentation, make sure you have constructed it with an opening, a body, and a conclusion.

Just as an architect draws plans when building a house, you want to design your presentation so that it is structurally sound. Audiences appreciate organization.

Including an Overview

Do audience members have a clear idea of what your presentation is about? What is your main message? Does the audience know where you are going?

Think of your presentation as if it were an adventure and you are the tour guide. Audience members want to know early on where you are taking them. Once they are informed of the direction in which they are headed, they can relax, settle in, and enjoy the trip.

Handling Media Interviews

The one time you must communicate absolutely, positively concisely is when you are being interviewed by a member of the media – especially on live radio or television. Reporters conducting live, on-air interviews are looking for brief sound bites (short answers to fit the tight time constraints of radio and television). Avoid long-winded, rambling responses. Answer the reporter's questions as directly and concisely as possible. Keep your answers short and to the point.

Summary

In today's fast-paced, impatient, and constantly changing world, communicating clearly, confidently, and credibly may not be enough to insure your success. You also need to communicate concisely and creatively.

To help yourself communicate more concisely, determine what messages you want to communicate to your audience. Then differentiate what would be good for the audience to know vs. what the audience must know.

Don't just memorize your presentation from beginning to end. Prepare different versions of your presentation to fit different time allotments. Have a five-minute version ready that includes the main theme, idea, or concept of your presentation.

You can add creativity to your communication by telling personal stories, using handouts, acronyms, and props. You can add clarity to your communication by organizing your presentations with a beginning, a middle, and an end. Including an overview will help your audience know where you are going and make it easier to go along with you.

Communicating concisely is particularly important when you are being interviewed by members of the media. Be prepared in advance to answer anticipated questions with short, crisp, and direct responses.

Remember to communicate clearly, confidently, and credibly—concisely and creatively, too!

ABOUT LEN LIPTON, PH.D.

*D*uring his career as a communications consultant, Dr. Len Lipton has delivered hundreds of presentations to audiences at international, national, regional and local conferences, seminars, and workshops on the topic of How to Increase Your Presentation Power.

Len has been a faculty member of the American Management Association (AMA), leading seminars on Effective Executive Speaking and Strategies for Developing Effective Presentation Skills. He has coached leaders in the fields of architecture, art, construction, education, interior and graphic design, insurance, law, marketing, medicine, public speaking, and real estate on how to enhance their presentation skills.

Len is the author of Knockout Presentations: How to Succeed in Business and Boost Your Career by Giving Sensational Presentations Without Fear. This reader-friendly reference book provides tips and techniques to help business people raise the level of their presentation skills to match the level of their areas of expertise. Len has a Ph.D. in Communications from the University of Southern California. He is a member of the American Society for Training and Development and the National Speakers Association.

Contact Information:
Len Lipton, Ph.D.
Presentations by Design
P.O. Box 1498
Santa Monica, CA 90406-1498
Phone: 310-451-5670
E-mail: lenlipton@earthlink.net
Website: www.lenlipton.com

HOW TO COMMUNICATE WITH DIFFERENT TYPES OF PEOPLE SO YOUR MESSAGE IS HEARD & APPRECIATED

by Doug Smart, CSP

Not too long ago I attended a party in the home of one of my neighbors, and I observed some interesting dynamics about how different types of people communicate. One of the women, a person who does not shy away from letting others know her opinions, boisterously vented such thoughts as, "The Thompsons had better keep their cat inside because I can't help it if my dogs decide to chase it up a tree," and "... so I told her, who does she think she is telling me I shouldn't let my kids leave their bikes in my front yard. I mean, this is America, right?" Heads nodded, some people laughed at her verve, and several others asserted their opinions, too.

Another large group congregated over by the fireplace, including a man who either knew everyone at the party or acted as if he did. He was overly friendly, told lots of funny stories (almost all of them included himself), and obviously enjoyed being the center of attention. Elsewhere, there were other groups, some rowdy, some low-key. Here and there were people who mingled in two's and three's and quietly shared laughs as they discussed their family travels and busy kids. Some engaged in earnest discussions about stocks, plumbing, and unfair traffic law enforcement. This occasion being a party, people congregated in clusters to have a good time. They tended to gather in groups that had similar communication styles. They communicated in ways comfortable for them.

As I looked around the room, I smiled. The scene confirmed something I had already learned: People like to be around people who have a communication style similar to their own. This observation leads to a very powerful truth: *To communicate more effectively, adapt your communication style to that of the person with whom you are communicating.*

All of us like to be around people who make us feel comfortable. And, as a rule, we tend to feel most comfortable around people who communicate and behave as we do. In 1928, William Marston published a book on the behavioral styles of people. He had observed that despite the complexities of human behavior, the way people behave falls into four broad categories that can be identified by the letters DISC.

D = Decisive, direct, ambitious, forceful, challenging, and a willingness to face problems and challenges head on. Some examples of D people are Senator Hillary Clinton, George Steinbrenner, Barbara Walters, and Karen (from the television show "Will & Grace").

I = Influential, imaginative, idea-oriented, optimistic, trusting, and an innate ability to influence others to their way of thinking. Some examples of I people are Bill Clinton and Jack (from "Will & Grace").

S = Steady, supportive, slower-paced, modest, sociable, self-effacing, with a preference for approaching their work methodically and at an even pace. Some examples of S people are Jimmy Carter, Charlie Brown (from "Peanuts"), and Grace (from "Will & Grace").

C = Cautious, contemplative, analytical, consistent, conforming, critical, and harboring a particularly strong fear of criticism. Some examples of C people are George W. Bush and Will (from "Will & Grace").

From the list above, does one seem to be more like you than the others? If you think that more than one aptly describes you, then between them, which behavior style is most like you when you are feeling stressed out or tense? That can be a big clue because, when we are under pressure, we tend to seek comfort by behaving in ways that are natural for us. That will most likely be your natural style.

Communicate Using the Platinum Rule

You can probably repeat the Golden Rule from memory. Do unto others as you would have them do unto you. Now take that wisdom to a higher level by saying the Platinum Rule: Do unto others as they would like to be done unto. Or in other words, treat people the way they want to be treated, not necessarily the way you want to be treated. Here are some general guidelines:

D people make up approximately 18 percent of the general population. They prefer you not make a lot of small talk or waste their time. If you have something to say, say it. They like to stay focused on the issue at hand. They want clear statements of the problem, its impact, and your recommendations for solutions. They prefer to make decisions themselves rather than being told what to do. The more intense the D factor, the better the ability to handle problems with quick action. D's are generally not afraid of saying yes to bold new ideas. D people like for you to be impressed by them, their abilities, and/or achievements.

Expect that 28 percent of the people you encounter in the general public will be I people. I's want to be recognized for their contributions. Frankly, they like personal attention. They enjoy conversation and fun. Even I's who are shrewd businesspeople readily acknowledge there is more to life than business. They like socializing, positive people, and "big thinkers." Your enthusiasm (or lack of) for solutions you recommend will influence whether or not they will accept your recommendations. ("If you can't get excited about this, why should I?"). Testimonials from people they respect will also influence decision-making ("If Tom Washington had success with your idea, then I know we will, too."). I people want to know the pertinent facts but do not want to get mired in the details.

The percentage of S people is the largest of the four behavioral styles. About 40 percent are S. They prefer a steady, predictable pace. They want you to take time to develop a relationship with them. S people want you to care about them and their situation or plight. Though they are usually warm and friendly people, skepticism is natural. The do not like surprises. Bold and risky ideas are scary and will need to be approached incrementally. They do not want you to rush them in decision-making. Besides the facts, they need to know how other people will be affected by the different solutions your ideas represent. They are sensitive to the feelings and potential reactions of others. S people want to know what you expect them to do. The more intense the S factor, the more the person appreciates your making a clear statement of what you think should be done.

C people comprise 14 percent of the population. They prefer you tone down emotional appeals and let the facts speak for themselves. Be practical. Like the D, they appreciate information and clear-headed discussion of a problem its consequences, and possible solutions. Unlike the D, the C wants more in-depth information and may require proof of the validity of your claims. C's also prefer taking their time in decision-making as it gives them time to consider various outcomes. The higher the C factor, the less they will like emotional appeals or be swayed by testimonials—unless they come from unassailable sources such as well-regarded research. C people want to be respected for their attention to detail, self-discipline, and thought processes.

A Shortcut for Identifying Each of the Four Behavioral Styles

Each of the four styles has a unique way of behaving that shows itself in communication.

DISC is all about observing behavior in others. Understanding your listener's behavior is effective because it allows you to appreciate "where he or she is coming from." This insight gives you an advantage many people don't know about—you can quickly see how to adapt to your listener's behavior and be more like him or her. For example, you don't want to be assertive if your low-key listener equates assertive with pushy. That could cause her to become defensive. And you don't want to be unassertive if your high-energy listener interprets deferential as weak and uninformed. That could cause her to feel you are the "wrong person" for her to work with.

You can discover behavioral style before you meet. Let's say you are getting ready for tomorrow's meeting with a prospect. You have never met the person but a mutual friend who made the introduction has. In order to plan a presentation that is a fit for your prospect's behavioral style, ask the friend "Is the prospect outgoing or reserved?" Listen for clues. D and I people are outgoing, high-energy, and readily express their opinions. They are extroverted. On the other hand, S and C people are more reserved, calm, and slower to reveal opinions. They are introverted.

Also ask, "Is the prospect more people-focused or work-focused?" I and S people take pleasure in the dynamics of relationships, such as small talk and the surprises of discovering commonalities ("We love to vacation there, too!"). In contrast, D and C people will grudgingly participate in chit chat but they take more satisfaction in getting the job done ("What I'd like to accomplish in this meeting is . . . ")

Putting the clues together can reveal a lot about your prospect, even before you shake hands:

Outgoing and work-focused = D
Outgoing and people-focused = I
Reserved and people-focused = S
Reserved and work-focused = C

Research shows DISC is universal: no matter where in the world your listener comes from, you will be able to recognize behavioral styles. The more you practice reading clues, the easier it is for you to distinguish between D, I, S, and C behavior and know how to respond appropriately.

How to Communicate Effectively with a D

D people are particularly good at solving problems. They prefer their information brief, to the point, and factual. They do not like time wasters and pointless chatter. They are assertive and might come across as intimidating to non-D's, especially if they are in power positions such as CEO or elected office or are wealthy.

How can you show a D that you relate to them—even if your own D factor is not particularly strong? And how can you "communicate D" with sincerity and not come across as phony or a light weight?

Recently, I ran a behavioral report for a client with a D score of 100. He was a top-of-the-chart D. As you might guess, he was a type A, hard-driving personality who was quick-tempered, dominating, competitive, and opinionated. He owned his own business (ironically, publishing children's books). If you were to call on him, how would you alter your communication style so you would be heard and appreciated?

Although some people find him intimidating, there are simple ways to get through to a "tough" person like this. His report included a section on how to communicate effectively with him. He agreed the tips on communication do's and don'ts listed in his report would make him happy. I'm going to share his lists with you. See how many of these you can do (or avoid) when trying to "sell" a D on your ideas.

Do:

- Plan your meetings (in this case, don't count on spontaneity to work in your favor)
- Get to the point right away
- Ask questions about his situation and what he wants to accomplish
- Identify specific ways your ideas will help him improve his situation
- Help him be more efficient
- Make your points with more emphasis on logic than emotion (but don't eliminate emotion—it's good to be passionate about what you are saying)
- Be specific about what you are offering and what you want him to do
- Ask for what you want
- Give clear choices
- Give an overview of how your idea will work if he says yes (don't give a detailed analysis—others will handle the details if he buys)
- Anticipate he will not be a sensitive listener (some D's are good listeners, many are not)
- If possible, provide a package of information that briefly summarizes what you are offering, benefits, mechanics, his/her role,

your role, and others' roles. This can be on one or two pages. You might give it to him at the meeting or deliver it at your second meeting.

- Use his terminology
- Use facts and figures to show probability of success

Don't:

- Talk aimlessly or waste time
- Repeat yourself unless necessary to make a point
- Fail to follow-up (He expects you to follow-up as part of the sales process, even if the first meeting doesn't go perfectly.)
- Get bogged down in details
- Assume he heard what you said
- Let disagreement reflect poorly on him
- Get defensive if he disagrees with you
- Argue
- Tell him what he should do
- Let him change the topic if you are not finished
- Be disorganized, scatter-brained, or uncommitted to your idea
- Let the D's air of arrogance turn you off. Stay focused.
- Try to change him
- Hang around longer than necessary for transacting business

How to Communicate Effectively with an I

Most of us would agree, I people are the most fun to be around. They look for ways to make work fun. They are effusive, enthusiastic, and demonstrative. They enjoy talking. They can get serious about business, but it doesn't take much to coax out their playful side. You will find they are usually the easiest people to sell your ideas to because they appreciate the excitement of new ideas, fresh approaches, and big-picture thinking. Plus, they are trusting by nature—visibly more trusting than the D, S, or C behavioral styles. But be aware, this does not mean they are pushovers for setting appointments with you or agreeing with whatever you want them to do. The secret to success with I people is in how you communicate with them.

Two weeks ago, I did a behavioral report for a super high I who scored 100 percent in his I factor. It included a section on "do's and don'ts" for communicating with him. He agreed; people who use those methods would get his full attention and respect.

As you read these two lists, think of your high I customers and how they would respond to the following.

Do:

- Be enthusiastic, upbeat, and positive about your ideas
- Let your passion for your beliefs show (I's understand the power of emotion.)
- Talk in terms of benefits—the more the better
- Keep the conversation moving
- Encourage his enthusiasm by listening to his ideas and asking questions
- Speak at about the same rate as your customer (which will be from brisk to rapid-fire)
- Use wit to liven things up and to show your cleverness
- Drop in clever, insightful observations
- Be brief
- Ask (often) for his opinions and ideas
- Use balanced logic in your presentation
- Be objective
- Use facts to back up your feelings and feelings to back up your facts
- Use testimonials from people who would be impressive to him ("You might be interested to know the great things Dr. Helene Carter at Memorial Hospital said about this program.")
- Point out his oversights ("One thing you might not have thought of is . . .")

- Talk in terms of solutions not problems. Help make her world better.
- Deliver a good verbal overview of what you are selling but deliver the details in writing
- Clearly ask for what you want and get an answer (otherwise you two can have a great time talking and later realize nothing was actually decided.)
- Be ready for the I to play "Devil's advocate"—which is a sign of interest, not the lack of it
- Be motivating, when appropriate ("People will thank you for doing this!")
- Set the stage for you to become a trusted advisor to your customer

Don't:
- Tell jokes that you wouldn't tell to a rabbi, priest, or minister
- Whine or focus excessively on problems (talk more about solutions than problems.)
- Out-talk him
- Act superior
- Be opinionated or closed-minded
- Be curt, stuffy, or repetitive
- Be boring, tedious or as predictable as a bad TV show
- Ramble
- Waste time
- Flood with details (he would rather see the big-picture view from 40,000 feet than to see the dirt on the blades of grass at 3 feet)
- Take advantage of his fun-loving nature by being patronizing
- Linger longer than it takes to transact business (or you'll be like relatives who overstay their welcome)
- Pretend you have to have all the answers

- Violate her trust
- Leave without an answer and/or an appointment to follow-up

How to Communicate Effectively with an S

With S people, niceness is a virtue. Over the years, if you have developed a long list of friends and customers who have stuck with you, chances are most of them are the S behavioral style. This is a reasonable prediction because the S style seeks personal and professional relationships that are deep and long lasting. The S favors steadiness, safety, and security—and long-term relationships meet that need. Once an S lets you into his or her world your place is assured as long as you don't cause substantial disappointment, in which case you will get a cold shoulder—either temporarily or eternally!

You can expect S people to be skeptical of new ideas and change. Building relationships they can trust is important, so you can expect S's to be slow-paced and casual about their time when talking with you (which can lead to longer phone calls and meetings). Also, they tend to withhold their true opinions until they have sufficient information to believe they are correct. When you ask them for a commitment, expect "Let me think about," "I have to talk with _____," or "I don't think so" until you have delivered enough satisfactory benefits that compel them to change their current routines and ways of doing things. (When you get one of those non-committal responses, you can nudge the process forward by asking in a supportive way, "What would be one or two concerns that could keep you from going forward?")

I went back through my records to find a DISC report I had done for a person who scored 100 percent in the S column. Here are the "do's and don'ts" for communicating with her that came from her report. She agreed; people who followed these tips would make a big impact on her. Think of the S people in your life as you read these.

Do:

- Show sincere interest in him as a person, his responsibilities, and his need to balance the needs of the various people who could be impacted by a "Yes" to what you are suggesting

- Be friendly but not overly-familiar
- Talk about how your ideas will help people your customer cares about. Be specific
- Give sensible, practical reasons for what you propose
- Stress the benefits others will receive if he says "Yes" when you ask for a commitment
- Take the risk out—as much as you reasonably can—by explaining the procedure if he agrees to make changes you suggest
- Use accurate facts and examples but stress the warm human side more than the cold numbers side
- Encourage questions
- Ask for opinions and about experiences with similar things
- Watch for signs of dissatisfaction or disagreement
- Give guarantees when appropriate
- Give references when you can

Don't:
- Rush the conversation (but you can use an agenda that carries the conversation forward at a reasonable pace)
- Brush aside emotional concerns as unimportant
- Patronize
- Take advantage of his or her niceness and try to bully a "Yes" answer
- Raise your voice or try intimidation to shake out a commitment (Even if you force a "Yes" answer, the person will not follow through and will have a bad taste from the encounter.)
- Make promises you can't keep
- Be disorganized or a person who "wings it"
- Exaggerate or use superlatives ("This is absolutely, without question, the most outstanding way to solve that problem!")
- Take offense if the customer wants to verify your information independently

- Mistake silence, nods, or smiles as agreement (It is common for S people to mirror the emotions of the person with whom they are talking.)
- Say, "Here is what I think you ought to do" unless you are specifically asked

How to Communicate Effectively with a C

Your C relationships want a few things from you in order to feel comfortable maintaining a friendship or doing business with you: an affiliation in which you respect and appreciate their needs, offer fact-based discussion, and give assurance that what you propose will actually work out the way you say it will. C people value precedent and have a built-in fear of new things not working out the way they are supposed to. It is good to talk about past successes in a factual (not boasting) way. They also want you to be organized in how you conduct yourself, rather than making decisions by the seat of your pants. The bottom line with C people: They want things to go well.

How do you communicate with a very high C so that you are heard and appreciated? Here are some tips from a behavioral report I ran for a top-of-the-chart C.

Do:

- As you prepare for a conversation, gather collaborating evidence that supports the validity of what you plan to say. You probably will not use all the information, but if you are asked penetrating questions you'll be glad you have it
- Be prepared but don't think you have to have all the answers
- Be friendly and supportive
- Be caring, candid, and open
- Give practical, solid evidence to back up your point(s)
- Assure there will be no surprises (as much you reasonably can)
- Give a step by step overview (written preferred) of what will happen if he says "Yes"
- Ask questions to discover personal goals, and then make a clear

link as to how your proposal will help him meet his goals

- Give him time to formulate and express his thoughts (C's tend to be slow, deliberate decision-makers because they carefully weigh the facts and merits)
- Watch for clues about disagreement or dissatisfaction (he might not verbalize negative feelings and later you'll be surprised he didn't do what you requested)
- List pros and cons of suggestions you make
- Follow through on *every* promise and commitment you make
- "Park" challenges and objections to which you don't have ready answers ("I don't think that will be a problem, but let me check on that and get back with you. Now, let's take a look at ... ")

Don't:
- Be sly or manipulative
- Rely on emotion to compel acceptance
- Use small talk after the initial greeting period
- Wing it or fake it
- Push for spontaneity (even if he admires it in others)
- Guess at answers. (OK to say, "Let me check on that for you.")
- Be all business. (Do show interest in him and his personal goals. Small talk is appropriate as a bridge to the real conversation.)
- Impose unrealistic deadlines
- Deliver your personal opinions as facts
- Make promises you can't keep
- Try to impress with your cleverness (If you need to make an impression, talk about the clever results you have gotten in the past.)
- Patronize or attempt to undermine
- Act in a less than professional manner
- Expect an immediate answer
- Say "Trust me!"

Summary

As you can see, each of the four behavioral styles has unique characteristics. In order to communicate well with each of the four, it is smart to observe the other person's behavior, identify the behavioral style that is most prominent at the moment, and adapt your communication style to more closely align with his or her style. If the person is fast-paced and task-oriented you want to express yourself as D-like, also, by getting to the point, not wasting time, and keeping an eye on the "bottom line." If the person is fast-paced and people-oriented, it is smart for you to also express yourself with an I-like quick pace, optimism and enthusiasm for the subject you are discussing, and recognition of the person's personal accomplishments. If you are communicating with an individual who is slow-paced and people-oriented, you want to adapt to an S communication style by not speaking fast or rushing the person to make a decision and by pointing out positive outcomes that will be experienced by others that he or she cares for if your listener agrees with you. If your communication is with a person who is slow-paced and task-oriented, be certain to provide your C with fact-based evidence to bolster your points, discuss both pros and cons of your ideas, and give practical evidence to back up your communication. You will find that by adapting your communication style to that of the people with whom you communicate, your message is most likely to be heard and appreciated.

ABOUT
DOUG SMART, CSP

*D*oug Smart is President of Grow Your Sales, LLC. He is a consultant and speaker who has presented over 2,000 paid speaking engagements around the world. He is the author/co-author of 15 books, including Sell Smarter Not Harder, Magnetic Leadership, Fantastic Customer Service, *and* 303 Solutions for Developing the Leader in You. *He is a Certified Behavioral Analyst and uses scientifically designed assessment instruments to help hire, develop,and retain exceptional people who are passionate about their work. In 1998 the National Speakers Association awarded Doug their highest earned designation, Certified Speaking Professional, an honor held by less than 9% of the 4,000 members. For three years Doug was host of the motivational radio show "Smarter by the Minute." He works with a wide variety of organizations.*

Contact Information:
Doug Smart, CSP
Grow Your Own Sales, LLC
P.O. Box 768024
Roswell, GA 30076
Phone: 770-587-9784
E-mail: Doug@GrowYourSales.org
Website: www.GrowYourSales.org

Resource Listing

Terry Adams, M.Ed.
Adams Consulting Group, LLC
74 Wheatsheaf Lane
Princeton, NJ 08540
Phone: 609-430-9971
E-mail: terry@AdamsGroup.biz
Website: www.AdamsGroup.biz

Dana May Casperson
The Power Etiquette Group
P.O. Box 3637
Santa Rosa, CA 95402
E-mail: danamay@PowerEtiquette.com
Website: www.PowerEtiquette.com

Connie Dieken
Founder & President
Communicate Like a Pro, LLC
Phone: 440-930-8500
Fax: 440-930-7555
E-mail: connie@communicatelikeapro.com
Website: www.communicatelikeapro.com

Mark Christopher Drury
9211 Hampton Ridge Court
Louisville, KY 40220-2982
Phone: 502-693-7598
Fax: 502-749-6608
E-mail: Markdrury@markgetsitdone.com
Website: www.markgetsitdone.com

Dovie Wesley Gray, Ph.D.
President & CEO
Wesley Motivational Training Consultants, Inc.
4115 Oxford View Court
Decatur, GA 30034
Phone: 404-284-5704
Cell Phone: 404-354-1755
Fax: 404-284-6524
E-mail: dovie@wesleymotivational.com
Website: www.wesleymotivational.com

Len Lipton, Ph.D.
Presentations by Design
P.O. Box 1498
Santa Monica, CA 90406-1498
Phone: 310-451-5670
E-mail: lenlipton@earthlink.net
Website: www.lenlipton.com

Natalie R. Manor
Natalie Manor & Associates (NMA)
Northeast Headquarters:
P.O. Box 1508
Merrimack, NH 03054
Southeast Headquarters:
317 Hickory Bluff
Johnson City, TN 37601
Phone: 800-666-2230
E-mail: CoachNatalie@NatalieManor.com
Website: www.NatalieManor.com

Kim Robinson
SMMarT Solutions
14052 Lakeshore Drive, Suite 100
Des Moines, IA 50325.
Phone: 1-877-840-7425
E-mail: Kim@SMMarTSolutions.com.
Website: www.SMMarTSolutions.com

Nan Siemer
BREAKERS
5906 St. Giles Way
Alexandria, VA 22315
Phone: 703-313-0147
Fax: 703-313-0172
E-Mail: breakers@erols.com
Website: www.BreakersConsulting.com

Doug Smart, CSP
Grow Your Sales, LLC
P.O. Box 768024
Roswell, GA 30076
Phone: 770-587-9784
E-mail: Doug@GrowYourSales.org
Website: www.GrowYourSales.org

Michelle M. Weil, Ph.D.
Human-Ware, LLC
Phone: 760-730-3894
E-mail: Weil@Human-Ware.com
Website: www.Human-Ware.com